CHAMPION DISC DOG!

CHAMPION DISC DOG!

THE ULTIMATE GUIDE TO GETTING YOUR DOG AIRBORNE IN 18 DAYS

MELISSA HEETER

Disc Dog World Champion and Professional Dog Trainer

CIDER MILL PRESS

BOOK PUBLISHERS

Kennebunkport, Maine

13-Digit ISBN: 978-1-60433-266-7
10-Digit ISBN: 1-60433-266-2

This book may be ordered by mail from the publisher. Please include $4.95 for postage and handling.
Please support your local bookseller first!

Books published by Cider Mill Press Book Publishers are available at special discounts for bulk purchases
in the United States by corporations, institutions, and other organizations.
For more information, please contact the publisher.

Cider Mill Press Book Publishers
"Where good books are ready for press"
12 Port Farm Road
Kennebunkport, Maine 04046

Visit us on the Web!
www.cidermillpress.com

Design: Alicia Freile, Tango Media
Illustrations courtesy of Shutterstock.com
Typography: Clarendon BT, Lino Letter, and Scala Sans

Special acknowledgment to Steven Donahue of See Spot Run Photography.

Printed in U.S.A.

1 2 3 4 5 6 7 8 9 0
First Edition

Acknowledgements

To the thousands of pet lovers who throw a disc for their dog, thank you for helping perpetuate and taking part in the one of world's most exciting dog sports.

To my many disc dog friends from coast to coast in the U.S., Canada, China, Europe, and Japan, thank you for your dedication to the sport, attending my judging and instructional seminars, buying my training DVDs, and spreading the disc dog sport worldwide.

Contents

Foreword

In 1997, Melissa Heeter made history by becoming the first woman to capture the Canine Disc World Championships after twenty-three years of male domination in the sport. Nowadays, Melissa travels the world with her amazing animal athletes, performing, instructing, judging, volunteering, and promoting the disc dog sport as well as educating enthusiasts from multiple dog sports how to physically condition their dogs and achieve peak-level performances.

I have long championed dog-friendly fun and games when dog training, and for me, nothing epitomizes fun in training more than dogs playing a game of chase, catch, and fetch with their owners. Without a doubt, it's the very best of activities for promoting the physical and mental well being of dogs and for enriching the relationship between dogs and their owners.

I first met Melissa Heeter several years ago at a dog trainers' conference. Melissa kindly offered to put on a personal demonstration for me. I watched in awe as she performed an amazing freestyle flying disc routine with multiple dogs. Her world champion dog, Ariel Asah, and her daughter, Ariel Ally, showcased a variety of synchronized jumps and catches that were stupendous and beyond belief (were they not happening before my eyes). As I watched the performance unfold, I noticed that the audience of dog trainers was growing until all the conference delegates were gathered around laughing and applauding. Now, it is not uncommon for dog trainers to disagree with each other regarding training methods, but on this afternoon, everyone agreed on one thing: These very lucky dogs were having the grandest of times playing (training) with their owner. Actually, it was difficult to determine who was having more fun—the dogs or Melissa. But not a person walked away after "the show" without saying, "Wow! I want my dog to do that."

Playing a game of chase, catch, and fetch with your dog is one of the most enjoyable ways to train your dog. For example, teaching "fetch" is perhaps the easiest (and sneakiest) way to ensure that your dog has a willingly reliable recall. You simply throw and your dog gives chase to catch the disc and then comes back to you. Your dog quickly learns that you cannot throw the disc until the dog has retrieved it. Delay throwing the disc each time and you will command your dog's absolute attention. In fact, wait until your dog sits for a while before throwing and then you'll have a rapid recall and a solid attentive sit-stay.

If you want to have ultra-mega-fun with your dog and train it at the same time, please do your dog a favor and read this book and learn Melissa's disc dog training secrets. And doggone it! Teach your dog to catch a flying disc.

—*Dr. Ian Dunbar, Founder, Association of Pet Dog Trainers*

Introduction:
Divert Fight into Flight

Dogs like to run, jump, chase, and bite prey, so through a simple game of fetch, a dog can become a healthy and happy companion for life. In the past, a dog's survival in the wild depended solely on whether or not he could catch dinner. Through thousands of years of domestication, dogs have been taught to depend on their human pack leader for their meals, which in today's busy world is usually a free bowl of food sitting accessible twenty-four hours a day. Therein lie the average dog owner's leadership problems and his or her dog's behavior problems. Free food along with a soft comfy couch and a fenced yard (where your doggie can bark at the neighbors to defend his own kingdom) is the perfect situation for a dog, right? Well, actually . . . no. A fenced yard is a good start for your dog's normal outside activity and safety, but placing a pack animal alone in the yard can be a cruel punishment to them, especially if there is little regular human interactivity. Plus, a dog should be reliant on their pack leader, their owner, for their dinner only after the owners eat as part of the family pack.

Handing our dogs' free food, letting them roam around the backyard and house destroying everything, and barking at people are definitely not the ways to have a successful companion relationship. Who walks in and out of the doorway first or gets in or out of the car first? It should be you, not your dog. Otherwise, who is in charge when the dog can do all of these bad behaviors? Yep, your dog is. Basically, if you allow your dog to do these things first then he is king and you are the servant. A bored dog has the potential to create his own jobs, and you just might not like the ones he chooses.

So, what does this all have to do with throwing a disc for your dog? Well, have you ever asked: Why do dogs like to jump? Why do dogs chase cats? Why do dogs like to bite and eat your shoes, socks, and underwear? Dogs are predatory animals and have several natural survival skills such as dissecting prey (toys), and strong hunting instincts ingrained in them. To a dog, a tennis ball is soft, squishy, and fuzzy and bounces erratically . . . just like a rabbit. A flying disc looks like a bird flying in the sky, and a tug rope (or your dog's leash) looks like and mimics snake movement. Throwing a disc is one of the most challenging natural games you could choose for your dog. Catching a disc in flight is like catching a bird. And when a dog learns the process of the fetching game, it truly gives him a natural, satisfying job—a successful hunt and kill. We just have to teach the retrieve.

I have been teaching dogs and their owners the benefits of this sport for more than thirty years. I've been lucky enough to travel the world showing people how rewarding this sport is, not just for the dogs, but for their humans as well. And I wrote this book so everyone can have a chance to learn to throw a disc to their dog, whether they just want more active time together with their pet or they want to compete in tournaments.

Inside you will find all of my training tips and tricks. From basic disc training to advanced competition techniques, this book is the one place to turn to begin this fabulous adventure with your canine companion.

A few reasons to play fetch with your dog:

▶ It will strengthen the bond between you and your pet.
▶ With pet obesity reaching epidemic levels, creating a consistent exercise program for your dog is a necessary step for overall health.
▶ It will strengthen your dog's mental and physical health and focus.
▶ A tired dog is a good dog. Daily exercise can turn your bad dog into a great companion.

Stalking a disc comes in many guises.

Before You Play

Even if your dog already fetches balls or discs, this chapter will take you through the proper discs to have on hand so your dog doesn't get hurt; the other equipment you'll need to have with you; safety concerns, including guidelines for the correct amount of time to throw and fetch a disc before resting; some general thoughts on training your dog; and much more.

All About Discs

I recommend purchasing ten or more 110-gram to 130-gram competition-approved dog discs made out of rubber, plastic, nylon, or polyurethane blend. Heavier discs (over 140 grams) aren't good for your dog's mouth and teeth, and cheaper brittle plastic discs tend to crack, especially in cold weather.

WHAT TO LOOK FOR

▶ If you can't bow the disc's top plate back and forth, up and down, don't throw it to your dog.

▶ If you throw the disc on the ground on its edge and it cracks or sounds hollow then don't throw it to your dog.

▶ The best discs starting from the top plate have a nice small slope down to the lip with ridges for easy gripping for your hand. Make sure the outside lip/rim shape is not too sharp of a curve—you want a soft, curved lip. The outside lip/rim should be more of a "C" shape, not a "V" shape. This is the part that touches the back of the dog's mouth on a catch, so rounder is better.

▶ If you're playing in colder weather (below 30 degrees Fahrenheit) use a flex, super-flex, rubber, nylon, or polyurethane-blend disc. They are safer choices for colder weather. Try to keep to the same size and mold during cold weather, as they will have similar flight patterns.

▶ For dogs that like to destroy the disc or puncture it while catching, try polyurethane discs, which are more durable.

▶ Discs come in various sizes, as do dogs. Make sure your dog can carry the disc in its mouth and not trip on it when he's running or walking.

Why Use Light Discs?

Light discs (110-120 grams) hover, float, and glide in the air when thrown properly, and these are the qualities you want when playing fetch with your dog. I always want my dog running, jumping, and vaulting (looking up while catching a disc). Your dog's mind needs to be free but focused to run, jump, time the disc catch at its apex in flight (looking up), and, once the dog has control of the disc in its mouth, he can freely look down for its landing.

Disc Diagram Description

A = Slope
B = Top Plate
C = Outer Rim
D = Inside Rim
E = Bottom Plate

The parts of the disc.

What happens when heavier dog discs (over 130 grams—with an average diameter of 9.5 inches) are thrown? The discs tend to drop rapidly in their flight pattern (descending down and forward like a jet plane), and the dog has to run full speed looking down into the ground. This is the same for smaller golf discs less than 8.5 inches in diameter with a flat top plate and no slope to the outer rim. I have seen too many dogs face plant, tumble, splay their legs and toes out, land on bended knees, and tip jump, landing on their rear unsafely with heavier discs. Your dog has only one chance to catch the disc and many will go all out head first. So, remember floating, hovering, predictable flight-pattern discs are more successful and safer for dogs as they have time to look up in the air, track the disc's flight pattern, and run and catch up to the disc.

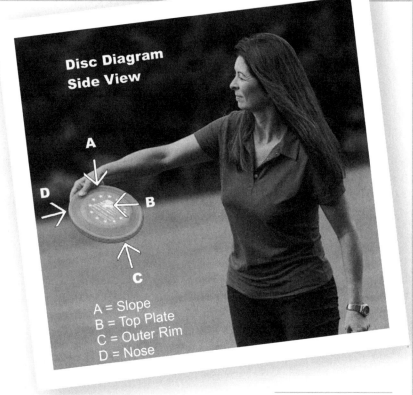

Parts of the disc, side view.

Disc Care and Maintenance

▶ The best method of disc maintenance is to sand or trim your discs if there are any bite marks, frayed edges, or puncture holes.

▶ You can also place all types of plastic discs in the dishwasher on NO-heat dry, or just stop the dishwasher before the heat cycle. This will reform your discs back to their original shape.

▶ If you leave your softer plastic discs in the direct sun or in extreme heat they will warp. Warped discs or discs with irregular (not circular) top plates or with puncture holes do not fly in predictable flight patterns.

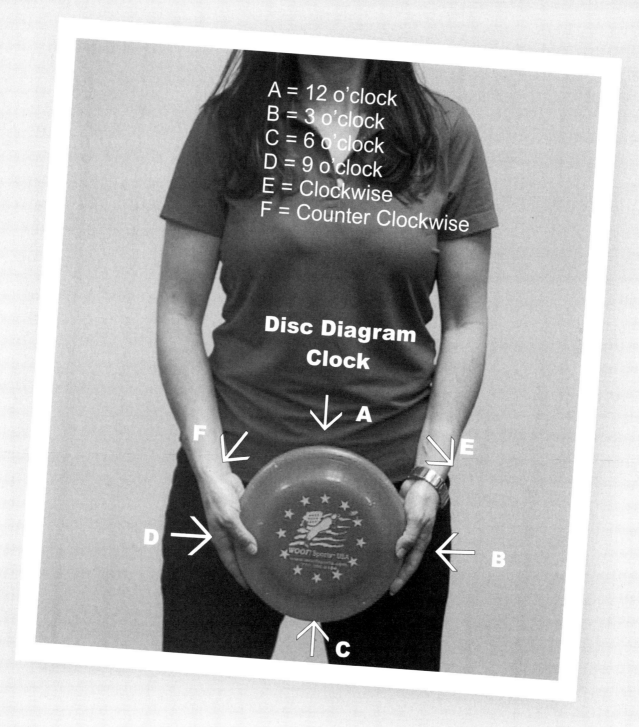

A = 12 o'clock
B = 3 o'clock
C = 6 o'clock
D = 9 o'clock
E = Clockwise
F = Counter Clockwise

Disc Diagram Clock

I use a clock face to describe disc position and hand placement throughout the book. Refer to this image for an example.

Other Equipment

Before you and your dog head out to the park for a practice session, you should carefully plan what disc dog paraphernalia to carry along. Many experienced enthusiasts consider the following items vital for any successful outing involving dogs and discs.

DEDICATED BAG

Keep a packed disc dog bag in the closet by the door. That way you can just get up and go practice without wasting time packing needed supplies.

Collar and Leashes

Dogs must be kept on leash at all times, except when practicing or competing. I also recommend that you keep your dog on a leash when near people, to avoid the possibility of an unfavorable encounter. I suggest a buckle collar to go along with a nylon or leather tab leash that's six feet long. You may also need a thin (1/2 inch) cotton training lead around twenty feet long when first teaching your dog to retrieve and come back to you.

Pooper Scooper or Plastic Baggies

Dog owners are required to clean up if their dog takes a nature break. Doing so demonstrates responsible dog ownership.

Towel

Use this for drying your hands and cleaning wet/dirty discs.

Tie-Out Stake or Kennel

Use either of these to secure your dog when not practicing together.

Water

Catching discs makes for a thirsty dog. Make sure you take fresh cool water to any event involving your dog. If your dog is panting hard, wait two or three minutes until he stops panting before providing water. Note: If your dog's tongue is curled up at the end like a spoon and he's panting heavily, your dog may be close to overheating. Take precautions and be an observant pet owner.

Lawn Chair and Shade Tent

These are necessary only if you're sure there won't be adequate shade at the park.

Cooling off after a hard day of play.

Safety

▶ Whether you are indoors or outdoors, you should never play on a hard slippery surface such as concrete, asphalt, hardwood floors, or tile without rubber bottom dog booties. Consider using Neo-Paws Orthopedic dog sports booties.

▶ Always play on a flat grassy area free of debris and obstacles or on padded carpet.

▶ Never play near a road with traffic.

▶ If your dog does not know "come here" never play off leash, always working on a twenty-foot-long leash.

▶ Inspect the field where you'll be playing for bottle caps, holes, uneven ground, debris, broken glass, and even sprinkler heads.

▶ Watch the weather and never play in extreme conditions. If it's 80 degrees or hotter, keep your dog cool by hosing him off before and after you train.

▶ As with any physically demanding sport, before you start training your dog, check with your veterinarian to make sure that your dog is old enough, physically fit, and able to engage in physically challenging activities.

▶ If working with a puppy, you can start as early as eight weeks; however, wait until he is twelve to eighteen months old before attempting any advanced moves or extensive jumping. A dog's growth plates usually close from twelve to eighteen months of age, so he should not vault off a person's body until after he reaches that age. He should also not be forced to jump any higher than he wants to on his own for a running-out catch.

Tips for Disc Dog Success

▶ If working with a puppy, it is a good idea to familiarize your pup to the dog disc at an early age, as young as eight weeks.

▶ Your first goal should be to teach your pup to retrieve the disc, take it out of your hand, track it flying in the sky, and love the game, so advanced training will come easy. Remember, that every dog is different and some can breeze through these lessons and for others, it will take longer.

▶ It is best to play in the morning, after your dog has just come out of a crate and loosened up and done his morning potty business, or when you have just come home after being gone for a while. (Generally speaking, your dog should be crated or otherwise separated from you for around two hours before training.)

Consider hiking, biking, or running for exercise.

Some dog trainers have doggy treadmills, which are great for building endurance.

▶ Always engage in play for exercise before your dog eats. Optimum feeding is thirty minutes after a workout. Never feed your dog and then work him, as the food can still be in his stomach digesting. Wait for at least six hours after he has eaten before a workout or vigorous play. However, I always work my dogs, and then feed them. I make them work for the food!

▶ When first introducing the sport to your dog, play for very short periods—five- to ten-minute sessions, three times a day. If your dog loses interest or refuses to play, you have played too long. The next time, cut the time in half, and then work your way back up by the next day.

▶ If your dog is excelling, always end the game with him wanting the disc.

▶ If you have an overzealous dog and you cannot control him, calmly lead him by the collar off the playing field and end the game, or walk away leaving him on the playing field. He will wonder why the game stopped. Just remember not to leave a disc with him, otherwise he may start stressfully chomping on the disc.

▶ One of the best ways to remember how long to play with your dog is however long you have played, he should rest double the time before playing again.

▶ Don't expect miracles right away. Like anything else, your dog learns through a natural progression of steps. Follow the lessons, and only move on once your dog has mastered each skill.

Training Tips

When training a dog for sports, you will almost always (99 percent of the time) use positive training methods. Also, what I have learned from training animals is to never say never. The moment you say *I will never use that type of training method*, or *I will only use this type of training collar*, you'll get a dog that needs that training method or type of training collar. My best advice is to find a trainer and training method that shows a positive improvement in your dog's behavior in a rather short period of time—especially if you have a dog with bad or seriously dangerous behaviors. Sometimes dog trainers and pet owners don't see eye to eye, so find one you trust. Communicating with your dog and understanding his physical, mental, and learning style needs are the secrets to success.

Now, in this book I do not have the space to dive into classical conditioning (Ivan Pavlov) and operant conditioning (John B. Watson and Burrhus Frederic Skinner), so don't forget to do some of your own research on different training methods when choosing one for you and your dog. Also, check out the trendsetting work of Karen Pryor, the clicker training queen, and her famous book, *Don't Shoot the Dog*.

Here are some training tips that will help you when working with your dog on tossing and fetching a disc.

HOW AND WHEN TO PRAISE

Understanding the power of praise is the most important thing you need to remember when training your dog. A simple "good boy" (or girl) or "yes," followed by a gentle pat and some happy eye contact are all you really need if you want your dog to repeat an action.

In the teaching phase of a new trick, never sound negative, and don't physically or verbally correct your pup in the learning phase. It is important to always use your dog's name before any positive command. If there is a change of commands, only use his name for

The one big exception to the 99-percent rule is if you have a dog that is repeating an undesirable or dangerous behavior. In that case, the most important thing for you to do is to stop the dog immediately from continuing that behavior. If you don't, the dog will come to believe this behavior is allowed and even think it is desirable. Dogs often reinforce themselves when the owner allows the dog to continue a behavior. One of the most effective ways to stop an undesirable behavior is to re-direct (re-command) him to lie down. And if he moves from the lying down position, you can correct him by gently placing him back in that down position. This redirection works extremely well for dogs that continually circle their owners and for dogs that spin just before they catch the disc.

the first command. This will reinforce his name and alert him a fun command is coming. That also means never using his name when correcting. Also, never correct a dog when he is learning a new behavior. Just stop and retry the command over or you can just walk away from the playing session. It is appropriate to correct a dog's bad behavior (such as biting), by saying "no sir" or "no ma'am" and gently grabbing the collar to avoid your dog from leaving the playing session. Always end on a good note with the dog accomplishing any simple task that he can if you get stuck.

Remember that your dog does not have a vocabulary and only communicates in the wild by reading other dogs' body language, tone of bark, body blocking, watching and repeating behavior, and intimidation. Our pet dogs learn through sight, smell, sound (whistles, clickers, other sounds), body language, hand signals, and finally the vocabulary we pair with all of the above. The only vocabulary your dog knows are the words we teach them through reinforcement. Don't overload your dog with commands. Start with learning three to five new commands a week, reinforcing each of them every day for just ten minutes a day.

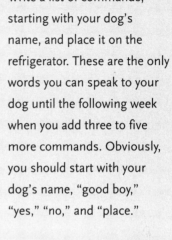

Having fun with positive reinforcement.

Rewarding Methods

Remember my motto: *"Through trust, exercise, and leadership, comes friendship."* The best way to earn your dog's trust is to become his caregiver. Feeding, bathing, brushing, walking, playing, and quietly bonding is the best way to do this. Every dog loves a good belly rub. Also, place the dog in a stand like for an exam at the vets, and examine him from his ears, nose, mouth, and neck to his shoulders, legs, and back. Your vet will appreciate it, and this time is well spent bonding with your dog in a calming fashion.

Be a Leader

The most important thing to remember in the dog/human relationship is that you are the leader of his pack. Your family and your dogs and cats are all pack members, so remember that in the wild, the pack leadership role can revolve between pack members. Make sure that you and all human family members are always the pack leaders. To gain more leadership in the family pack, use the down-stay command or make your dog wait before going out the doorway.

Create an Exercise Program

Create a consistent exercise program such as walking daily, fetching a ball, fetching a flying disc, or playing obedience recall games with food. You can even teach your dog to walk on a treadmill for those cold and rainy days. A tired dog is a good dog, and a simple game of fetch can turn your bad dog into a great companion.

The author and Viola the rescue dog.

"Through trust, exercise, and leadership, comes friendship."

—MELISSA HEETER

General Training Techniques

In order to have a successful disc dog experience, it's important to have several training techniques on hand. And even though this is not a general training manual for dog owners, I've included a few methods you should know how and when to use: luring, shaping, capturing, redirecting, withholding, and stopping.

LURING BEHAVIOR

Luring has been used in competition obedience to lure the dog into positions. It's also used in dog agility—luring the dog through, onto, or over obstacles has been the most successful way for new dogs to learn agility obstacles. The luring method can be used with food or with any motivational object your dog likes, like a tug rope or Flyball.

Shaping Behavior

Shaping can also be luring your dog to learn many different behaviors that may take several small steps to accomplish a difficult task. This is used when teaching difficult routines to be used in dog sport competitions or in training service dogs, like at the Canine Assistant Dog Institute. These routines can be time consuming, so shaping the behavior in stages with food is the most successful way for the desired end result.

Capturing Behavior

When would capturing a behavior be a benefit in training? If you have a dog that likes to stand up on his hind legs, try this: When feeding your dog his daily meals, hold his food bowl just up to his nose level and slightly raise it to his standing nose level. As a reward for him standing up following the food bowl, pair the phrase "stand tall" with one hand raised up as if you were raising your hand in school for a

question. While your dog is standing tall, lower the bowl slightly so his head is tipped down and let him take a few nuggets. If you need to, you can hold one paw to help your dog balance. This is a great core muscle building exercise. Don't forget to pair, or capture, the dog's behavior with a command. In no time at all your dog will start offering this behavior other times. So, just command him to stand verbally and give a hand signal, and say "yes." This is called capturing at this point.

Re-directing or Re-commanding Behavior

Re-directing is a good choice when you want to stop a dog from repeating an undesirable behavior. If a dog learned to spin while catching a disc, you can redirect him by commanding him to down. This method works exceptionally well for spinning. So by redirecting your dog to a down position, the dog is corrected. Now, this method also stops the dog from continually making the mistake of spinning, so it is dual-purpose training. The dog can continue playing with you by starting over on the toss and fetch starting line. However, you must redirect your dog to down by walking over to him and commanding "down" every time your dog starts to spin. It is important for your dog to continue playing after you stop him from spinning. It is also important that the dog learn that you want to play with him, but the spinning has to stop before you can continue. So, the dog must problem-solve to understand that when he spins without a command that behavior actually stops the playing. Once he understands this, your training becomes easy.

Withholding and Stopping Behavior

The withholding and stopping method of training is a successful way to communicate to your dog not to continue a particular behavior. For many instances in disc dog, withholding and stopping go hand in hand. In obedience you can withhold food and reward the desired behaviors. You can do the same with the disc. A good example when to use the withholding method is when a dog is catching multiple discs in a rapid throwing sequence and refuses the first disc because it wants the following discs. This is usually a display of too much prey drive and a lack of bite (or commitment to bite). It could also be a lack of commitment to make decisions. So, if a dog refused the first disc of a multiple sequence, pretend to throw the first disc by moving your hands from low to a high as if you were going to actually throw the first disc, but do not throw it. This withholding and resetting/starting over is the most effective way to communicate to your dog the throws do not continue until you catch.

Understanding Motivation

Understanding what motivates a dog is also important to consider when training a dog for sports. Food-driven and object-driven dogs are the best for toss and fetch; however, you can train just about any dog to catch a disc and bring it back to you.

FOOD DRIVEN

Dogs that are food driven are excellent candidates for any sport. Their behavior can be lured, shaped, captured, or redirected extremely easily. It is easy to test if your dog is food driven just by placing some dry nugget food on their nose and luring them around. One rule of thumb though, is that there is no food involved at advanced levels of canine disc sport, and at some point, the dog should understand that praise and the disc are their rewards. If you have a dog who is just not interested in looking at a disc, then feeding the dog out of the disc is a good place to start for the socialization period, but the food should be taken away quickly and it is best to get the dog tugging on the disc as a reward.

Marni Brown and Quin in a mid-chase leap—driven to catch the disc.

Object Driven

Any time a dog is object driven, he can usually be driven by more than one object. In canine disc sport, you want the dog to understand that any object *you* have is the one to desire. So, place a high value on the discs, especially the one in your hand. If your dog is truly object driven, he will catch a disc thrown by anyone. Object-driven dogs can learn by luring him to do an action, and then rewarding with that object.

Obstacle Driven

One of the best examples of obstacle-driven dogs is an agility dog. These dogs love to perform each obstacle as fast as they can and the need for speed becomes the motivation. Any agility dog that is truly obstacle driven will run a course with anyone.

Pat Hanley and Scout demonstrating weave poles for obstacle-driven dogs.

People Driven

Dogs that are people driven are what are usually called people bonded. This is usually always considered a good trait. If your dog is people bonded, then he chooses to focus on you and not on other objects or obstacles, possibly even food. These dogs just want to please you and can be lured by simple verbal or physical praise. This is a plus when training for obedience, but sometimes they are too focused on the person's face to even look at any other object or obstacle. On the other hand, a people focused dog is a perfect choice for the average pet owner, too.

Dog Bonded Dogs

Dogs that are bonded to another dog usually make great companions as a second dog. They tend to keep each other company and typically do not get into too much trouble. The best way to create a human bond with a dog-bonded dog is for you to create some special time with only that dog. It could be taking that dog for walks, or becoming its caregiver, creating some special games, or even teaching him to fetch. This bonding time will help communicate to your dog that you are his companion and he needs to look to *you* for leadership, friendship, and play time.

Chase Driven to Another Dog

Many herding dog are chase driven to other dogs or to live prey such as birds, squirrels, bicycles, or even cars. A dog that displays chase-driven traits that has not been taught to stop on command or to not chase dangerous things like moving automobiles usually ends up getting seriously hurt or killed. So, the first and most important thing you need consider is some serious anti-chasing training.

Where Your Dog Is Coming From

I believe it is important to understand your dog's predatory fight, flight (flee or escape), and freeze responses before you begin training for toss and fetch. The basic predatory responses of the canine can be used to "divert fight into flight"—which is diverting a dog's predatory responses onto the *flight* of the flying disc. My motto is, "the flying disc gives a dog the most natural instinctual job they were bred for, which is STALKING, RUNNING, JUMPING, CHASING, and BITING an object."

▶ If you have a dog with strong-to-excessive characteristics in stalking, chasing, and/or biting, then you have a dog with a stronger **Fight** response at some level.

▶ If you have a dog with a strong **Flight** (flee or escape) response, then your dog lacks the confidence to accomplish one or all of the stalking, prey drive, chase, and/or bite behaviors. However, this is not such a bad problem, just a minor confidence situation that can usually be overcome.

▶ If you have a dog with a **Freeze** response, then he makes no decision to fight or flee on his own in a difficult situation, but chooses to stand still because it is frightened, insecure, or does not understand.

If you have a dog with a strong flight response (a flee or escape behavioral response) or a freeze response, I strongly recommend slowly building up your dog's confidence. Teach your dog to trust you and the game by stalking, chasing, and biting the disc for fun. Play tug of war with a disc by teaching your dog bite it. Then give a drop command. If your dog will not drop the disc, bring out a second disc. Other options are when the dog returns to you, do not grab the disc immediately, but rather pet the dog vigorously all over his body, as a fun positive response for retrieving. (Playing tug of war is only recommended when you are building drive in a dog with a flight or freeze response.)

So, the dog with the Fight response will be able to tunnel his fight instincts into STALKING, RUNNING, JUMPING, CHASING, and BITING the flying disc, whereas the dog with the flight and/or freeze responses will be able build confidence and thus make an all-round more confident dog.

Melissa and Faith stalking the disc.

A well-rounded disc dog has strong stalking, prey drive, chase, and bite. Some dogs or breeds have plenty of prey drive, but no prey chase. Others have plenty of stalking, prey drive, and chase, but no bite (prey-kill instinct). Still others have such a high prey-kill instinct that it takes over and your dog ends up "killing" the flying disc. And then there are the dogs that lack the confidence to accomplish the stalk, prey drive, chase, and bite traits at all and have been taught by their owners to focus on their face or eyes and not on the object they are playing with. So, make sure you place a high value on the object by having fun and looking directly at the object in the teaching phase. If your dog has any lack of retrieval skills, go back to the retrieval basics and concentrate on praising every step the dog gets right. If he gets any step wrong, go back to kindergarten and break down each step to find the problem. If your dog has a lack of focus, you can play a keep-away game with a second person (throwing the disc to each other with the dog in the middle). It is important to put a high value on the disc that you are playing with and let the dog accidently intercept it by rolling or throwing by the dog, not directly at the dog. This helps the dog understand that he can actually get the disc and that if his owner wants the disc, he should want it as well.

TRAINER'S TIP

I do not suggest playing keep-away on a regular basis, but just as a training technique to get your dog interested in the disc. If keep-away is played for too long it can make your dog too aggressive with the disc, panic when you take the disc away, or have the opposite effect of not being interested at all.

Remember, that any dog can learn to fetch something. Just make the game fun for you and the dog. Also, if your dog likes to bark, jump up, use his paws, chase, or bite too much, he has the potential to become a fetching machine. An important factor to remember is that almost all breeds of dog today still have plenty of prey-chase in their instincts. So, whether he is chasing a ball, flying disc, or chasing you back to the starting line of a Canine Disc toss & fetch competition, all dogs will speed up if you run the other way. So, use that in your fetching foundational training. By getting involved in the Canine Disc Dog Sport, you will experience the wonderful, exciting, devotional new-found bond with your canine companion. It will also turn your bored, bad, backyard dog into an interactive member of your family. Your dog can't speak to you in words, but he does communicate through behavioral responses and actions. I will never forget the old dog trainer saying for when a dog does an undesirable trait: *No more complaining, but more training.*

Basic Training— An Eighteen-Day Program

In just over two weeks from now, your dog will be fetching discs thrown by you on a consistent basis. Simply follow the steps in these five lessons, all of which build solid foundational retrieving skills, and you and your dog will be enjoying a new game together— one that will strengthen the bond between you. From getting used to the disc to jumping and catching a disc, these lessons take you through the basics up through mastery of basic catching skills. Advanced techniques follow in the next section of the book.

Lesson 1: Focus Play/ Familiarization Days 1 through 4

Y ou first want to test your dog to see what level of focus play or prey-drive he has. To test your dog you will need a corner of a room, or a hallway.

STEP 1

1. Face the end of the hallway or corner and place yourself three feet from the end of the corner.

2. With the collar and a thin six-foot leash attached to your dog's collar, place the dog on your left, one foot behind you. (For each step of all of the lessons, your pup will start on your left in the same position slightly behind you, unless otherwise stated.) You should be facing the corner or end of the hallway for this exercise.

Step 2: "Get It"

1. Place the disc upside down at first in your throwing hand. As your dog progresses, change the disc to right side up and move it along the ground.

2. Drag the disc flat on the floor like you are scrubbing the floor. Work up to sliding the disc on the ground and say "Fido, get it!" (Use your dog's name, of course.)

3. While dragging the disc, you will look at it, thus placing a high importance on it.

4. If the dog goes for it, looks at, or touches the disc, praise him joyfully with your voice. You want the dog to make physical contact with the disc by either using his mouth or feet. The more he touches the disc in any way, the more praise you should heap onto him.

5. You will only do this five times per individual training session.

6. Once your dog is consistently touching the disc, you are ready for movement with a release. You can repeat your sessions as often as you want, but do not do so many that your dog quits or loses interest.

TRAINER'S TIP

In the beginning, always roll or slide the disc away from your dog and never throw it directly at his face. You don't want to frighten your dog with the disc.

Step 3

1. With your dog on your left and the leash still attached, take the upside-down disc and drag it on the ground, saying "Fido, get it!", but just when the pup goes for the disc, gently release the disc into the corner.

2. Repeat this process five times.

Cara Hutto and six-month-old Jedi.

Feeding and watering your dog out of a dog disc can teach him that the disc is fun, friendly, and one of his toys.

3. Your pup should do one of several things: go for the disc, go for the disc and touch it, go for the disc then lose interest, look at you and not the disc, just sit there and ignore you and the disc, or try to run away. You can keep the pup involved in the disc or at least with you by kneeling on the end of the leash, trying to keep him focus playing with you and the disc.

4. If the dog touches the disc, encourage him to "get it" by saying it again and dragging it around some more.

5. If your dog loses interest, drag it around again and look directly at the disc saying it again. Keep doing this until you get him to look at the disc.

6. If the dog looks at you instead of the disc, look at the disc, pick it up and show it to him and drag it around and saying "get it!" again.

7. It may take a few times for him to realize that playing with the object means playing with you. If your pup refuses to do anything, make him accomplish some little command he knows like sit or down, then praise that and end the game.

Lesson 2: Retrieving into a Corner with a Roller Days 5 through 9

1. Step back six feet from the corner you were playing into in Lesson 1.

2. With the leash attached to your dog, take the upside-down disc and gently release the disc, scooting/sliding/rolling it six feet away and say, "Fido, get it!"

3. Repeat this five times.

4. If the dog picks it up, but does not bring it back, use the leash to gently reel him in with the disc in his mouth.

5. When he returns, *do not* take the disc from him. Simply verbally and physically reward by saying "good boy/girl" and petting him vigorously anywhere but his head until he drops it. "Good boy/girl" is now part of every training session when he does a good behavior.

A roller beginning throw release point

A roller released.

Step 2: "Get It—Go" and "Here"

1. With your dog on your left and the disc in front of him upside down, scoot, slide, or roll the disc into the corner and say, "Fido, get it—go!"

2. Once the dog has the disc in his mouth, say "here," while clapping your hands on your legs while reeling him in with the leash.

3. If he does not pick it up, repeat "get it," while going back to the focus play of dragging it around. Continue looking at the disc and dragging the disc around until the pup picks it up or touches it.

4. When the pup finally returns, *do not* take the disc from him at this stage. Just verbally and physically reward by saying "good boy/girl." Pet him vigorously anywhere but his head until he drops it.

5. Repeat "Fido, get it—go, here" five separate times.

Step 3: "Get It—Go, " "Here," and "Drop It"

1. When teaching the phrase "drop it," it is important to pet the dog vigorously when he returns. Also, don't reach for the disc at this stage or offer him another disc to tug on when he returns.

2. If, when you reach for the disc, your dog starts a game of keep away, then play tug when he returns.

3. Now, at the appropriate moments, say "Fido, get it—go," "here," and "drop it."

4. If the pup won't stop playing tug of war, then do not reach for it, but pet him vigorously rustling him all over or alternatively have another disc and waive it around looking at it yourself and make it more fun so he can tug on that one to drop the first one. Then say, "go, drop it" and waive the second disc around. You have to teach him that the name of the game is GO, GET IT, HERE, DROP IT. GO, GET IT, HERE, DROP IT. GO, GET IT, HERE, DROP IT, again and again. Once he learns this, you can have a fetching machine and some fun exercise together.

If your dog loses interest, try playing keep away, throwing the disc to another friend, while your dog watches. When your dog shows interest, float or roll a disc past him allowing him to intercept the disc. Give your dog lots of praise for each attempt. Never allow your dog to chew on the disc like a chew toy. If he won't drop it, bring out a second disc and play the trading game. You can also teach tug and drop on command.

Step 4

1. Now, head outside and roll the disc on the ground at greater distances in the same fashion.

2. You will now start to proof your retrieving distances with scooting or rolling a disc.

3. Attach a long leash to your dog's collar for retrieving training, letting it drag on the ground.

4. After he chases down the disc, call him, "Fido, here."

5. If he forgets the disc, gently tug the leash to get his attention and tell him "Fido, get it—go, here."

6. If this doesn't work, gently pull him back to you while praising him. Running the other way helps your dog want to run toward you.

7. Once your dog has mastered this lesson, try cutting the leash in half, until there is no leash left and he gets the idea of retrieving with the disc.

Lesson 3: Take It and Catch Training Days 10 through 12

STEP 1: "TAKE IT" FROM THE STAND-STILL POSITION

1. Now, head outside to a flat grassy area that's from five to ten yards square.

2. Your dog's starting position is on your left, three feet behind you while facing his running field. Meanwhile, you're turned sideways so he can pass by the front of you. You can stand or kneel for these next steps so your dog is always seated to your left to running passed you to your right, i.e. the playing field.

3. Hold the disc right-side up with your throwing hand and touch it with your other hand several times and say "take it."

4. If your dog does not take it, then go to focus play, dragging the disc on the ground and saying "take it."

5. If your dog still does not take the disc, become more animated with your voice and actions to show your dog how much fun he is missing.

Taking the disc from a stand.

6. You can always reach down and gently touch the leash to help your dog start moving.

7. Repeat this process five times.

8. Work your way up to releasing the disc just before the dog takes it. Do not forget to verbally and physically reward by saying "good boy/girl" whenever you see a behavior you like.

Step 2: "Take It" from the Run

1. Stand your dog about three feet behind you on your left (so he can pass by you) while holding the disc right-side up with your throwing hand, touching it with your other hand several times. Say, "take it."

2. If your dog does not take it, then go back to focus play, dragging the disc on the ground.

3. Immediately go back to "take it."

4. Next, move the disc from low to high as if the disc was going up and down an elevator (vertical). The disc should only move one plane at a time. Say "take it."

5. If the dog won't take it this way, hold the disc at a level horizontal plane about a foot higher than the dog's head and run in a straight line away from the dog and have him take it from a horizontal moving position.

6. If your dog picks up on the vertical "take," move onto the horizontal plane with you running away from the dog holding the disc so he can take it out of your hand. This is the beginning stages of learning to leap. Don't forget to verbally and physically reward.

Taking the disc from a run.

A one-plane (vertical) throw.

A two-plane (horizontal and vertical) throw.

A longer two-plane throw.

7. Repeat the vertical exercise five times as one segment and then move on to the horizontal running takes. For future training it is important that your dog know how to take a still disc out of your hand at some level, so make sure your dog can accomplish this step. It sounds simple, but it's necessary for future commands.

8. Once your dog can do both vertical and horizontal running takes, add them together and use two plane takes.

9. Start stationary, while lowering the disc down, and when you move it up, walk forward adding the second plane of horizontal motion to the disc.

10. Once your dog has the one vertical plane from low to high, you can add the second horizontal plane or adjust their stride or even do a restrain release where another person gently holds your dog until you say "go." This will create more prey drive and motivation to want the disc more.

Step 3: "Take It" Over the Body

1. For this step, the dog stays two feet behind you, on your left facing you, while you move in front of the dog's running path and sit on the ground with your legs extended straight out. You want to sit in front of your dog as if you were stretching to touch your toes, so he will have to jump over you to get the disc.

2. Hold the disc right-side up with your right hand (directly over your knees so your dog has to jump over your legs).

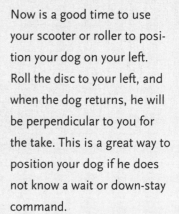

TRAINER'S TIP

Now is a good time to use your scooter or roller to position your dog on your left. Roll the disc to your left, and when the dog returns, he will be perpendicular to you for the take. This is a great way to position your dog if he does not know a wait or down-stay command.

Jumping Puppies

Do not ask a puppy to jump any higher than his chest level until he is four months or older and do not repeat too many times. Between eight and twelve months, you can follow your dog's nose height for levels of how high he can jump one session every two weeks (which should consist of no more than ten jumps in one session). However, I warn you do not overdo it. Your dog's growth plates usually close from twelve to eighteen months, so if you do too much you can risk injuring your young dog.

However, you can teach your pup to jump up onto your bed from a sit position. This is a softer landing zone and your pup will learn how to use his legs as shock absorbers. When your pup is eight to ten months old, you can even have your dog jump over a hurdle onto the bed. This is safe and teaches your dog how to control his body in the air.

One of my favorite jumping training techniques is to play a game where my eight-month pup jumps from my arms while I hold him and say "ready, set, jump." Let him jump up freely from your arms onto a soft bed mattress. My dogs love this game and really learn to use their legs to cushion their landing on the soft bed.

Touch the disc with your left hand several times and say "take it." You now have become an obstacle he has to jump over.

3. Remember, that you are still starting the takes with the disc moving in one vertical plane first. Repeat "take it" while throwing the disc (flat-hovering) straight up two feet over your knees.

4. Now, have the dog start from either side of you by having three discs and teaching the dog to "take it" from the left, from the right, and then left again. Say "take it" for each throw. This is also a great time to teach an overzealous dog to wait, by withholding the disc (moving it out of the way quickly so he cannot take it), if the dog goes before you say the command. Graduate to a throw, in one vertical plane over the body, like the elevator moving straight up.

A one-plane throw over the body.

Lesson 4: Tracking Rollers and Mid-air Catches Days 13 though 15

STEP 1: LEARN THE ROLLER GRIP

A roller is where the disc rolls on the ground like a wheel away from the dog.

1. Hold the disc in your throwing hand with the bowl side away from you, your hand on top of the circle of the disc (like a car steering wheel), your fingers on the inside of the disc, and your thumb on the top plate of the disc facing your chest.

2. With the disc's position in the center of your chest, roll your hand clockwise starting from 12 o'clock to 6 o'clock, snapping the disc to your right.

3. When you release the disc on the ground it should be released at around a 45-degree angle to the ground, since it will otherwise tend to curve too much to the right.

4. The actual release starts by bringing your thumb to your chin, bending at the elbow only. The disc should be vertical now with the top plate facing you. Snap your wrist down to the ground, so the disc lands three feet away from you and rolls at least five to ten yards in a straight line away from your dog. The disc should roll in a straight line to your right, away from your dog's running path.

The only other roller I recommend is a roller for puppies. This is where your hand is at the bottom of the disc at 6 o'clock and the bottom plate is facing the center of your waist. Curl the disc and touch your forearm and snap your wrist to the ground so it rolls to your left. It is important that the disc rolls in a straight line when the puppy catches it. If it curves too much or sharply, then the puppy, who is not fully developed, has the potential to have his head and shoulders go one way and his butt and hind legs go the other.

Roller grip.

Step 2

1. Grip the disc in a roller grip. Say "Fido, get it-go!" and snap the disc, so it rolls at least five yards to your right (the dogs running field). Keep his focus on the disc before it leaves your hand.

2. Use your focus play training and make him use his retrieving skills.

3. Use the long line to reel him back so he does not run off.

4. Repeat this process five times.

5. On the third day of this session say, "Fido, go!" and from then on. As he accomplishes retrieving rollers at five yards, double the distances every couple of days. To test his tracking skills he should always come from behind the disc chasing it away from him. This is to make sure that he tracks the disc when it leaves your hand. If he anticipates and takes off too early, do not throw it. Bring him back to starting position and start again. For adult dogs, you can do rollers a far as you want as long as the retrievals are good and your dog keeps focused.

6. The secret to having your dog come back to you is to run in the opposite direction when your dog gets the disc. Dogs just love the chase game and will run back faster to you if you are running away from him. Once you have rolled the disc about five yards away and the dog gets the disc, turn around, with your back to your dog and run away while calling your dog's name, "Fido, here." You can clap your hands and look back at your dog, but by running away the dog should want to chase you.

7. At this stage, your dog will want to at least get the disc. If he does not bring the disc back to you, place your dog on a long line and start the exercise over. The long line is for you to grab and bring the dog back into you. So, the exercise starts the same, with a roller and running away, but before you start, unravel the long line and throw it between you and your dog, so it can drag behind your dog as he runs out to get the disc. This way when the dog runs past, you can easily reach down and grab the long line as it drags between you and your dog. Once your dog has the disc in his mouth, pick up the line as you turn around and run away from your dog reeling him into you to make the fetching a success.

8. Slowly increase your roller lengths when your dog becomes proficient at the last distance. Always make sure that your dog has eye contact with you and then the disc before you release it. It is important to praise profusely for successful efforts. Never scold a dog for failure to retrieve the disc. Just do not say anything if the dog does not retrieve it. Remember, canine disc play is a team effort!

Rollers from the ground.

A word of caution: Do not overthrow the disc to your dog on a regular basis. Some dogs with low to medium drive will learn they cannot catch up to the flying disc and it could hinder their drive.

Step 3: Mid-air Catches

1. You will now be throwing the disc at distances so your body position is important. You will be sideways as if about to take a golf swing. Stand or kneel for this step, but make sure the dog can pass you by from left to right to catch the disc.

2. Grip the disc in a backhand throw (see Lesson 5 on page 59). Start by lowering the disc to the ground and then raise it up and throw it straight up floating completely flat. Say "Fido, go!" and snap the disc upward, so it floats up in one vertical plane, as if the disc is going up an elevator. The throw should be two feet in front of his face, so he has to choose to MOVE to the disc to catch it. Don't throw it at him. This is introducing motion (mid-air catching) to the disc and he will now have to time his running catch.

Melissa and Airen demonstrating a one-plane vertical beginner throw.

Cara Hutto and Jedi demonstrating a two-plane throw.

3. In the beginning, make it as easy as possible by placing the disc about two disc widths away from his mouth, then throw it five feet, ten feet, fifteen feet, ten yards, and then twenty yards down the field. Try only throwing the disc on a vertical plane at each distance (of five feet, ten feet, fifteen feet, and then ten yards) at a time before adding two planes of the disc moving in a vertical and horizontal plane. Repeat each distance five successful times before moving to the next, then repeat that and so on.

4. For further distances, continue doubling the distances as long as he makes mid-air catches and you make good throws. Never try to throw farther than you can control the disc.

5. Once you hit twenty yards, stay there for a long time. Then mix one long throw with several twenty-yard throws, always mixing up the length of throws.

If dog has a problem releasing a disc during toss and fetch, try using two discs for a while. Send the dog out for one disc and then when the dog returns trying saying "go" again. Do not throw the disc until he drops the first one, but this way you are redirecting the dog to what he actually wants, which is to chase and catch another disc. Your goal is to get the dog fetching one disc, then having him run around you and getting another disc, and repeating the fetching sequence. So, if you have to offer your dog a second disc for a while that is okay in training. You play the two-disc trading game by always throwing the second disc you have for a while, then, when the dog has this down, you will reach down and pick up the disc he dropped and throw that one, even though you have a second disc in your hand. So, now you should change the variable of one time throwing the second disc and one time throwing the one the dog retrieved. You will then graduate to taking only one disc to the field, and by now the dog should know that he only gets to fetch the one he retrieves.

Have a stack of discs ready for when the dog returns to you.

Lesson 5: The Grip, Stance, and Motion of Throwing
Days 16 through 18

My rule of thumb is that for every one throw you make for your dog, you need to practice five times more throwing without your dog. For this training exercise you will need five to ten discs and a flat and grassy playing area that's a minimum of ten by forty yards. You will learn the backhand throw, which is the throw you will most often use when playing toss and fetch with your dog. For advanced throwers, throw into some kind of netting with a rope or ribbon box with a three-foot square marking the center. This will help give you a target to look at. The net should be about fifteen feet by fifteen feet in diameter. Start by standing fifteen away and move back, progressing only when you can hit the square center box consistently.

STEP 1: YOUR STANCE AND GRIP

1. Start by standing parallel to the long side of throwing field, like a golfer about to tee off. Distribute your weight so two-thirds is on your back leg and one-third on your front leg. (All descriptions are for right-handed throwers).

2. Place the disc upside down in your left hand (non-throwing hand).

3. Take your pinky and ring finger and grab the lip of the disc and rock the disc back and forth on those two fingers with the disc hanging straight down.

4. Now, tighten your pinky and ring finger, so the disc ends up directly into the palm of your hand.

The relaxed backhand grip.

5. Close your hand like you are shaking a pair of dice, and place the disc in your hand. Then place your first finger on the outside of the disc and with its knuckle wrapping down around the bottom of the disc. The most comfortable position for your middle finger is close to the ring finger, either facing down toward the other two fingers or also tight against the rim of the disc.

6. Place the disc bottom (bowl) on your legs, holding the disc with both hands at 9 o'clock and 3 o'clock (with 12 o'clock being the top of the disc closest to your chin).

7. Rotate your right hand around the clock of the disc to 5 o'clock and touch your right forearm with the rotated disc letting go with your left hand.

8. Make a circle with your arm where the disc still touches your right forearm and raise the disc in front of your left (opposite) shoulder. This is what I call the serving platter.

9. Now, lower your right hand three inches lower than your shoulder.

10. Keep the disc in the curled position, now so it almost touches your throwing forearm.

The standard backhand grip.

The power backhand grip.

by inch just like that lawnmower cord unwinds with your arm stopping at shoulder height pointing to your right. Stop your hand straight at your target.

11. Wrap (coil/curl) up your disc inside your arm so it makes a circle in front of your left shoulder.

12. Keep the disc almost touching the center of your throwing forearm and still keep your arm in a circle in front of your left shoulder. Make sure your curled wrist is lower than the opposite of the disc for the correct angle, in the stance position.

Step 2: Your Throwing Motion

1. Now, imagine you're pulling a lawnmower cord with one quick tug/pull of the arm from left to right. Your hand needs to unwrap inch

The backhand starting position.

2. Your hand will need to snap to the straight position with your fingers facing forward and all pointing directly at your target with your palm facing toward the ground. One of the tricks to remember is that the throwing motion starts from the knee first, and then moves to your hip, then lead the throw with your elbow and finally end with the snap of the wrist ending shoulder height with your hand facing palm down.

3. Release the disc at a slight angle so it will spin to a flat position for the dog to catch. If you bend over slightly at the waist directly forward and looking at your toes you'll have the correct angle.

4. On the finished release, your weight distribution shifts from two-thirds on the back left leg to two-thirds on the front leg with a slight swivel/twist of the hips from left to right.

5. The best way to get better is to take twenty discs and throw them without your dog down the field, and then go pick them up and throw them back to your starting position. This is the quickest way to learn and helps you deal with different wind directions.

Conclusion

So, that's it—all you and your dog need to do to successfully create a lifelong bond and a game your dog will never tire of. Whenever he forgets a piece of the training, go back to that step and re-teach it. And don't forget to be consistent with your training and to keep at it. Don't go too long between sessions, even if you have to do some focus play during bad weather.

Next up are advanced techniques you can teach your dog for fun or if you are considering competing. Good luck!

▶ If you hold onto the disc too long, it will hook to the right, which means you did not have enough vertical angle on the disc when you released it. So, remember that the bottom plate on a backhand throw is always facing your body. Bend over at the waist more, looking down at your toes, for the correct angle.

▶ If your disc goes up on your release, then you faced the nose of the disc to the sky on the release or you put too much palm of your hand on the disc.

▶ If your disc went up, then you pointed the nose of the disc straight up on the release.

▶ If your disc went left you let go too early, and if your disc went down, you released too low or from the waist.

▶ The nose of the disc is two to three inches down from your first finger. The disc always goes where you throw the nose of the disc. The disc will fly where you point the nose.

▶ On almost all throws, pull straight through your stroke of the disc and finish with your chest to your target. Only when you are advanced should you add a step to your throw or follow through your arm past your body. In the beginning, always stop your hand or fingers directly at your target.

▶ You control the distance of your throw by how much snap you place on the disc.

▶ If a disc wobbles close to your hand within five to ten feet, you are either not holding the disc tightly enough or you're holding it too tightly. If the disc wobbles farther away, then there is usually not enough spin/snap on the disc to continue carrying the disc through the air.

▶ When you want to throw longer distances past forty yards, reach back behind you just before you coil (wrap the disc up) and start your throwing motion. The reach back can help you add another five yards. Remember that you must look at your target first as your body starts the throwing motion. So, the motion is looking first, then knee, hip, elbow, and wrist snap. Another secret to longer distances is to add a step just before you throw. It is also important to drop your left shoulder after the release and throw more of an arcing throw, like a backwards "C."

See page 147 for more throwing styles you can experiment with.

The Distance Backhand Throw.

This sequence shows the backhand stance and motion positions up to the release point.

Advanced Skills and Tricks

Once you have the basics down with your dog, you can move on to more complicated tricks and games. The drills in this section will also help solidify the training already accomplished.

Games That Build Skills

Once you start playing toss and fetch games with your dog, you can easily build more drive in your dog for running back to you.

1. Take two discs onto a large field.

2. Place your dog on your left as have been doing while training.

3. Roll the disc on the ground, using a backhand roller, away from your dog in a straight line.

4. Follow him, running out for about five yards, and just before he catches the rolling disc, turn around and run back to your original starting spot. Dogs love the chase game and will run back faster if you are running way.

5. Once you've done that for five times or so, try this. Repeat steps 1 through 3 and when your dog retrieves the disc, wait until he's about five yards from you, and then say "drop" and roll the second disc away from him in a straight line so he has to run past you. This is called a passing game, and you can use it to proof your dog's retrieval levels so he'll bring a disc to your feet, drop it at different distances, focus on another disc, and then go back to retrieving at your feet. Keep changing the retrieval games to keep it fun for your dog, but always go back to a few fetches to your hand or feet for proofing your retrieval.

6. Run back and pick up the first disc, which your dog dropped to fetch the second disc, and throw it again.

7. You can roll or throw discs in this passing game as many times in one session as you would like. However, it is important to always end or begin each daily training session with a simple single disc toss and fetch game, where the dog must fetch the disc to you all the way.

Recall Game and Retrieving Drills—Restrained Recall With and Without a Long Line

1. Start with two people standing ten yards from each other. Both should have some smelly, yummy treats.

2. Before starting the game, make sure the dog knows that you both have treats. Stand or sit facing each other and, one at time, take turns calling your dog to you, by saying "Fido, come."

3. If your dog starts coming to the person before the second person calls, then that person would turn away and the other person would call the dog back to him or her.

4. You will want to work up to thirty, forty, and even more yards away from each other. You can even add more people to the game. Just make sure that you only play long enough so the dog stays interested.

5. Once your dog loves this game and you're standing farther away, have the one person call the dog to them and then turn and run away, calling the dog once more. When he comes give him the treat.

6. To take this to another level, have one person gently hold the dog and the second person run away calling, "Fido, come." This game is best done with a tug rope (like a five-foot-long Flyball fleece tug), a thrown tennis ball, or a disc.

TRAINER'S TIP

Only play this passing game once your dog understands the single-disc retrieval game. If you play passing too much or add multiple discs into the fetching game before you have proofed your single-disc retrieve, a dog can easily forget that the retrieve is important, too.

An advanced passing game—running back to your starting position.

Increasing Prey-Drive & Chase

1. Have a friend gently hold the dog as if the dog is on the start line. Make sure he is about ten feet behind you and on your left.

2. Stand in your throwing position and look at your dog, then say "Fido, go."

3. In the beginning, the person gently restraining the dog will easily let go of the dog, but as the dog advances, in a week or two, you are looking for the dog to pull a little on the person holding them and then shoot out of their hands when he hears "Fido, go."

4. Only restrain the dog for a few weeks and alternate with a down-stay send out. A word of caution: If you choose to place your dog in a down-stay, you MUST look at your dog and release with "Fido, go" clearly and loud enough so your dog does not make a mistake and still stay when you intended him to go.

The starting position for recall to another person.

Different Toss & Fetch Starting Positions

I t is best to teach these positions with treats separately from the disc. You can lure, shape, or mark the position with food to get your dog in the correct position and then reward.

FRONT POSITION

This is used for almost everything in freestyle flying disc. This is where the dog sits in a perfect front sit position, facing you, at a distance of about one of the dog's own body lengths. This is easy to teach.

1. Start with the dog somewhere in front of you and lure the dog with treats pointing with both hands at their nose while stepping backward.

2. Bring your hands closer to your chest while you are stepping back and say "front."

3. This command is the secret to success in canine disc. Your dog can start so many tricks from this starting position. Just about everything I do begins and ends from a front position.

Melissa and Faith in the front position.

Playing with multiple discs in the front position.

Down-Stay

This position is where the dog is in a down-stay two or three feet behind you on your left so the dog can relax and calm down until you say "go." So, ultimately your dog will be parallel to the long side of the playing field, but perpendicular to you, so he can run past you.

1. Just guide your dog to a down stay with food often in everyday live, giving them a flat hand signal (palm to their face) and say "down-stay."

2. Only reward with food once your dog has went to a down, then again when you say "stay."

3. You can add this down stay command to your disc play once the dog responds to it consistently.

4. On this starting position, it is most important that you look at our dog and connect, making eye contact, and then say "go" when you are ready.

5. If you do not reconnect with your dog, then the dog might miss your command and still stay or false start.

Jake in the down-stay position.

Shay Zerm and Coley in the middle position.

Middle Position

This is a starting command that sets up your dog for any sport. The most successful competitors in canine disc or dog agility have a start command that will make a connection with their dog in a close proximity. The middle command is also used for teaching many freestyle disc tricks.

1. The middle is a great place to start and then you give the stay command and move to a different starting position by saying "middle, down, stay."

2. Then walk two to three feet away from your dog, look at him and say "Fido, go."

3. You must reconnect with your dog by looking at him, making eye contact, then looking at your throwing field and saying "Fido, go."

Close Position

This is a left heel position and is also a great command where the dog is facing the same position as you. Once your dog knows the close position, you can teach him to do just about anything. This starting position is the most commonly used for right-handed throwers for a send out.

1. Teach your dog the close position by using food and lure them to walk behind you, on your left side.

2. Then step forward and reward your dog when his right shoulder is on the center line of your left leg.

Melissa and Faith in a close position stalk.

John Everly and Tucker hiking in close position.

Side Position

This is a right heel position. Remember, that a heel position is where the dog is parallel to you, facing the same direction as you. We use this in freestyle a lot for sending the dog around counterclockwise or preparing your dog for any maneuver from right to left of your body. This is used for left-handed throwers for the most successful send out.

1. Once your dog knows the side position, start with him in a side position and step forward about two or three feet.

2. Then throw a sidearm throw with your right hand. This sidearm throw will rotate to a flat position and have the high side of the disc to the dog as he is running and catching. This is a trailing-away throw with lots of angle and has a counterclockwise spin on it so it will rotate to a flat position and an even rotation to the high side to the dog's mouth.

3. This does two things: It teaches the dog to catch trailing away throws and also teaches your dog to leap for the disc as the disc will have the high side of the disc to the dog's mouth with the counterclockwise spin.

Glory in a side position.

Disc Exchanges

A disc exchange/send out is when a dog starts out on retrieval or comes back from a retrieval. Each one of these send outs can be taught with food and then with a disc thrown as a reward. However, a few words of caution: Some dogs are too driven to the disc. This can make a dog lunge and try to still the disc. So, the most successful way is to start with food and teach the dog each command individually. Once he knows them, you can move to using the disc. Some dogs do just fine starting with the discs. So, this can be a trial and error of what works best for your dog.

Faith handing off the disc to Melissa on a disc exchange.

The Around

This send out is the favorite of many handlers. This is when you start with the dog in front and send the dog around your body clockwise for a retrieval. This is the best send out for a right-handed thrower. On this send out, when the dog comes around clockwise he can look back over his shoulder and track the disc easily before, during, and after the release.

Pat Hanley and Scout in the around position.

The Circle

This is where the dog starts in front and goes around his handler counterclockwise. This is the best send out for left-handed throwers. One of the easiest ways to teach this is to use food or a disc and lure the dog around your body as you turn counterclockwise, saying "Fido, circle." Once the dog has this with food you can move to using a disc and then throw the disc as the reward.

Tanner Williams and Edward demonstrating a side position leading to a circle send out.

The Through

This can be used for a dog that has a wide clockwise outrun if you send them around from there. This through will usually cut a dog's outrun in half. Starting from a front position, the dog runs between your legs and exits to the left coming back around clockwise to the throwing field. So, this is more like a 180-degree run through that turns toward the running field.

Pam Hanley performing the eight send out.

Shane Williams and Chess demonstrating the through send out.

The Eight

This works best if you are a left-handed thrower and you have a dog that has a wide counterclockwise outrun. Starting from a front position, the dog runs between your legs and exits to the right coming back around counterclockwise to the throwing field. So, again, this is like a 180-degree run through turn in back toward the running field. This method also seems to cut the dog's outrun in half and redirects him more easily to the throwing field.

The Spin Go

This worked best for my world champion dog, Ariel Asah. She only wanted to come back just long enough to give me the disc and go out again and again. So, it was easiest for her to come to my front position, slightly to my left side. She would hand me the disc in my left hand, then she turned 180 degrees clockwise and I said "go." This also worked well for her as she was one of those border collies that would get stuck in a counterclockwise flank (circle) as I redirected her into a spin go.

Melissa and Glory in a spin go.

TRAINER'S TIP

It is nice to have your dog hand you the disc, but do not demand that your dog hand you the disc all of the time or too often. He may stress out and start not coming back close enough. Worse yet, the dog may start chewing on the disc as a stressful indecision.

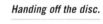

Handing off the disc.

Matra is jumping up and handing off the disc.

Catching Multiple Discs

Once your dog is retrieving single discs reliably, you can move on to teaching him to catch multiple discs. If you've been playing with one disc for a while, your dog may not drop a disc to catch another one. Here's how to solve this problem.

1. Place the dog on an upside-down bucket or a mini trampoline. The best buckets to use are the old style metal garden tubs that are about thirty inches in diameter. Make sure the bucket or trampoline is on a non-slippery surface. (Many dogs can start on the ground staying in one spot and not moving forward or around you, but once a dog learns to catch multiples while moving forward it is difficult to teach them to stay stationary. So, I teach stationary multiples first.)

2. Have from three to five discs in your hand and hold them in front of you while facing the dog.

3. Start with a backhand throw that's angled to your right. Say the command "catch" or "take."

4. Once the dog catches, tap your discs together and say "catch again."

5. Your goal is to get the dog to catch the first disc, then look for a second disc, catch it, and so on.

6. When your dog has mastered the right angle, then move the discs to the center, and then to the left angle. If your dog can catch up to five discs with a right, center, and left angle, without getting off the bucket or trampoline, then you can speed up the tosses.

7. Once your dog has mastered different angles and different speeds on the bucket, then you can move to flat ground.

Ready for more than one disc!

Have a special movement with your hands to show the dog if the disc will be thrown to the right, left, or center. For example, when throwing to the right, your hands should be shifted to the right of your body holding the discs at a steep angle. For right to left throws or side to side multiples, your hands should move from left to right and then throw in the right position. The dog will see the motion and get in the rhythm of your hands. For medium- to slow-speed throwing, start with your hands at your waist and on the throw, for your right angle, bring both hands up slightly during the throw and then back down again. The up and down motion of the discs in your hand will show the dog the direction that the discs will be flying, which starts from low and moves to high for the catch. The left arch and right arch are the same. Flat throws are best held still and then shuffled out like a deck of cards where each disc that you throw touches the next disc. Always shuffle and throw the discs in a multiple segment from the bottom of the stack. When holding multiple discs in your hand, hold five discs vertically in your left hand and bounce them so they fall fanned out, pinching the bottom in your left hand. For faster throws, try tapping the disc together just before the first disc is thrown.

Multiples Gallery

Alena delivers a unique upside-down multiples sequence by lying on the ground.

Behind the back!

Melissa and Asah: multiples into a shuffle, with great disc management preparing for the next throw.

Monomi Konishi and Liaka demonstrating a kick off the chest.

Marketa Urbaskova and Chuckie demonstrate a unique shoulder stall, balancing on her hands, with a multiple delivery.

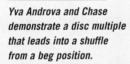

Yva Androva and Chase demonstrate a disc multiple that leads into a shuffle from a beg position.

Grip and Bite Drills

Bite and grip work is extremely important for freestyle disc dogs as competitors throw many different grips and releases to their dogs during a freestyle routine. It is easy to spot a dog that has not been taught how to catch clockwise, counterclockwise, and inverted discs as the discs tend to spin out of the dog's mouth or bounce out. Here's how you can proof your dog's ability to catch clockwise and counterclockwise spins.

GETTING USED TO INVERTED DISCS

1. While facing your dog, throw the disc upside down. This helps the dog get the feel of the inverted disc in its mouth. Inverted discs not only feel different in a dog's mouth, but they also fall differently while in flight. A dog tends to leap and jump properly when catching an upside-down disc. As his head reaches down in mid-jump for an upside-down disc, his rear legs collect and follow his body forward. This is not normally true for right-side up discs as they drop differently in their flight patterns. This is most likely because an upside-down disc falls away slowly, and as it falls, the dog is trying to get on top of the disc; however, a right-side up disc tends to fall at a much faster speed, so the dog is still in his prey-chase (running) mode and not in their jumping/leaping mode.

3. Now, try a two-handed spin with the disc right side up as a direct throw to your dog's face. In the beginning, all direct throws need to be slightly off-center advancing to directly center throws with the dog's experience level.

4. To really proof your dog's bite and grip on the disc, throw a two-handed floater clockwise and counterclockwise, (right side up and upside down).

Asah and Melissa demonstrating an upside-down delivery to a back flip, which helps teach the dog to reach back to catch the disc.

Lucka Schonova and Dixie performing a kneeling chest vault delivered upside down.

Melissa and Asah performing a chest vault delivered upside down.

Butterfly Spin

Another way to proof your dog's bite on the disc is to throw a butterfly spin to your dog. This is also called a third-world spin where the disc spins end over end directly in front of the dog.

1. Place disc upside down in your hand with all four fingers on the bottom of the disc, which is the top plate facing the ground.

2. Now, place your thumb on the top of the disc, which is the bottom of the disc facing the sky. Your hand will be at 6 o'clock on the disc, which is closest to you.

3. Place your elbow firmly into you right side and move your hand waist high to the center of your body.

4. Bring the 12 o'clock part of the disc to your chest and now snap the disc down to the ground. The goal is to have the disc flutter down toward the ground and have the dog move to the disc to catch it.

The butterfly spin throw.

The butterfly spin throw.

Spinners

Spinners are another way to test a dog's bite on a disc. This disc spins sideways in a left to right spin.

1. Gripping the disc with your pinky finger on the left side of the rim and your thumb on the right rim place your index finger on the bottom plate. The top plate needs to face the ground.

2. Bend your two middle fingers toward your palm. Now, spin your wrist to the left like you are flipping a pancake.

3. The trick to this spinner is to use your little finger as the last part to touch the disc and spin the disc off of that little finger. Your dog should be in front to start and the most successful way to start is to hold your dog's collar with your left hand and teach them to reach out with their mouth.

TRAINER'S TIP

In the beginning, your dog will have a better chance catching the disc when it's slightly off-center. However, for an advanced dog, directly center is best. And the faster the snap the more likely the dog will catch the disc.

A spinner.

Jumping Drills

Jumping drills are one of the most important training drills you can teach your dog if you want to work on advanced moves or even compete in Canine Disc. This is because dogs normally use two-thirds of their front body to jump and have to be taught to use their hind end properly. Many people think that a dog's jumping ability can't be improved, but in fact, dogs can be taught to be a safer and more versatile jumpers. You can teach your dog to use his hind end and shift (tip) his hips directly under his body more before he jumps. This helps your dog with the collection (final stage of his jump). You can also teach your dog to enjoy jumping more, to feel comfortable in the air during a jump, and how to handle his landing. When watching a dog jump, it is important to consider the four elements of the jump: pre-jump (shifting), air time (body control in mid-air), post jump (landing), and how to move out of a jump.

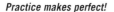

Practice makes perfect!

Hurdling

This first exercise is to teach your dog to jump over one low jump.

1. Set an adjustable hurdle at your dog's nose.

2. Stand alongside your dog with your dog starting in a sit-stay.

3. Run with him as he jumps over the hurdle, keeping your shoulders parallel to the dog's running path and forward movement.

4. Then, teach your dog to jump from a sit, one body length away from the hurdle. A body length is the length from your dog's chest to the end of his butt.

5. At the beginning, your dog should start from a straight line and land in a straight line, from one body length away from the hurdle on both sides of the hurdle. Once your dog has accomplished his hurdle at his own nose height, move the hurdle bar up in two-inch increments. A typical jump practice time is about ten jump sessions before moving the hurdle bar up to the next height.

Chris McLeod and Calico display the finished result of hurdling work with a nice start line sit-stay.

6. A jump session is dependent on your dog's age, but a good rule of thumb for a dog eight to twelve months old is one jump session twice a week, which includes five to ten jumps in each session.

Jumping Muscle Memory Skills

Building muscle memory skills are also important. Do this by adding two and three jumps together in a straight line. The suggested jump height for a beginner dog is his own knee height. For the best results, your dog needs to be at least twelve to fourteen months and able to jump their own chest height before adding multiples hurdles together.

1. The dog's running line is perpendicular to you, so he can pass by you to the hurdles.

2. When figuring out the hurdle distances, it is important to estimate your dog's running stride, starting with one full running stride between each jump. The jump distances between each jump hurdle should start at least one-and-a-half of your dog's body length.

3. To perfect your dog's running and jumping technique, move the bars up in two-inch increments before adding more running strides between the hurdles.

4. Once your dog has accomplished three jumps together for ten sessions at chest height, your dog is ready to add a disc to the equation. Any time your dog moves up a level in height or stride, remember to only move either the height or stride first.

5. Place three jumps together, with your dog in a sit or down-stay, ready to jump the straight line jumps. You can also have another person hold your dog in a restrained recall starting position for this exercise. Go to the end of the jumps, on your dog's right side. Command your dog to jump by staying "Ready, set, go, over."

6. At this stage of the jumping drill, your dog should land after the last jump and make one running stride before catching a floater. The goal of this jump sequence is to teach your dog muscle memory of adjusting his stride by starting at the same stride distance between the hurdles at first.

Mid-air Adjustments

Jumping and adjusting in mid-air are important for a versatile jumping dog. Many dogs are not comfortable jumping and need to be taught the mechanics of jumping. So, try this exercise.

1. Place your dog in front of the hurdle, with your dog on your left. Step forward to the bar and pivot around facing your dog so your shoulders are parallel to the jump bar.

2. Standing on the left side of the jump, leave enough space for the dog to jump the hurdle and land and turn 180 degrees between you and the hurdle. It is best to use food for this exercise as a disc or toy can be over-stimulating at this point.

3. Command your dog to jump the hurdle, saying "over," luring him with your right hand over the jump and then between you and the jump pole. This teaches flexible jumping and teaches your dog to turn and wrap in mid-air while watching for careful landings.

4. Move to the other side of the hurdle and repeat.

5. When practicing both left and right turns this will help teach your dog to adjust his body in mid-air and increase your dog's flexibility. This is also the perfect time to add the phrase "over right and/or left." Don't forget that it is your dog's right or left when commanding left and right directional.

The final result of true agility and flexibility is displayed in this jump.

Mid-Air Adjustments with Jumping Disc-Drop Game

This exercise will have your dog take an upside-down disc, while you lower the disc down about six inches from your original disc-holding (stationary) position, as he jumps over a hurdle. The secret is that the dog must be in mid-jump, focusing on the stationary disc and then, while the dog is in mid-air, lower the disc six inches. Dogs are quadrupeds, and when the head moves from high to low, the rear will follow. When the dog's head reaches down to catch the lowered disc, his back will round and his rear end will collect underneath for a safe landing. Remember, that you are only moving the disc in a one vertical plane, like an elevator going up and down. Not only does this exercise teach your dog proper jumping styles, but it also builds confidence in your dog's jumping and teaches him to jump up and take the disc. Jumping up and taking the disc is very important, as many dogs learn the bad habit of waiting until the disc falls to the ground to retrieve it.

1. Straddle the hurdle bar with your dog perpendicular to you and the jump bar, so he can pass by you on his jump. Hold the disc upside down, higher than you want the dog to jump.

2. Let your dog jump up and over and lower the disc while he is in mid-air.

3. Repeat the exercise three to five times.

4. Next, stand beside the hurdle, opposite of the dog, and about two to three feet away. Have the dog repeat the previous exercise, taking the disc while this time, you hold the disc a little higher and then lower the disc six inches again while the dog is in mid-jump. Let him take the disc out of your hand even though you are lowering.

5. Repeat three to five times.

6. Your goal is to slowly move away from the hurdle having your dog take the disc at more advanced heights and distances away from the hurdle.

7. Each exercise should be at the same height three to five times from a sit, then a stand on all four feet, and then at a run before raising the hurdle height.

8. Once your dog has mastered taking disc drops at different hurdle heights from a sit, stand, and then a run, and at different distances, then you can start moving the disc horizontally (adding a second plane of flight).

9. A successful jump is smooth on all three parts of the jump: the leap (which is lift off), mid-air (which is hang time), and the landing.

In mid-air!

Dog Catch

A dog catch is an important way to bond, reward, and reconnect with your dog. Your dog needs to know that you will catch him and feel comfortable in your arms, so you'll start by sitting on a sturdy stool, an armless chair, or even an old short tree stump. This exercise is best when you use treats and hold your dog successfully in your lap for at least ten seconds without your dog struggling.

1. Encourage your dog by luring him with a treat to jump into your lap. Start with your dog jumping up from your left to your right while you say "come up" and tap your treat hand to our chest. Hold your treat hand turned with the treat and your fingers facing your face at an arm's length away from your face. This way the dog will jump up and look at the treat. Many dogs that jump up in the beginning, jump up and tip their head back, possibly hitting you in the chin. So, it is best for them to jump up and look away from your face and at your hand.

2. If your dog only uses his front paws and does not jump up, pick him up and place his hind feet onto your lap. Do this until he is comfortable.

3. The next progression is to straddle the stool in a squatting position, which looks like a sit, and work your way up to a slight squat, leaning back a little with your dog jumping into your arms. If your dog will still not jump into your arms, use a taller stool for practice.

4. Your goal is to make this game fun so your dog will trust that you can catch him, and like to jump up to bond and reconnect with you as a reward.

Tanner Williams teaching Edward the beginning dog catch.

Teaching the dog catch from a sitting position.

Teaching the dog catch over a hurdle for proofing.

Dog Catch Gallery

Steven Heeter and Radical Rush, the 1994-96 World First Runner-Up.

Laura Moretz and Cubby competing at the Disc Dog Southern Nationals.

Melissa and Faith performing a dog catch from a flip.

It's important to teach your dog in a sitting position before attempting to catch them while he's jumping for a disc. When you surprise a dog that has not been caught before, it can lead to undesirable negative impressions of the trick, and many dogs will not repeat it. Some dogs are so surprised that their natural survival traits come out and they can even snap, growl, or fight to get down. So, always use patience and work at your dog's own speed when teaching a trick in which he has to trust you. Caution: Only catch a dog that is comfortable jumping up in your lap first, and if the dog's weight is close to sixty pounds you must be able to comfortably catch him.

Advanced Dog Catch

Start with your dog jumping over a hurdle into your arms without a disc and then once your dog is comfortable jumping into your arms over the hurdle, add a disc.

1. This is the same perpendicular starting position (to your dog), so your dog is facing the jump bar and looks like he will pass by you, but you will reach out and catch him while luring with food up over the hurdle into your arms. Your dog in on one side of the bar and you are on the opposite side of the bar.

2. The dog catch is easier if you stand while slightly squatting down with your left leg (hip distance apart) a little in front of your right leg. This helps keep you centered so you can gently squat down during the dog catch.

3. When using a disc, start where your dog jumps from left to right, into your arms, and have your dog jump over the hurdle and take a disc out of our hand.

4. The most successful right-hand position is to hold the disc upside down and grab the far side of the disc (which is 12 o'clock) with your fingers on top of the rim and your thumb on the bottom of the disc.

5. Now, stretch your arm out as far as you can, leaving your elbow still bent some. This method works great as your extended arm will catch the dog's chest so you can scoop up the dog's rear end with your left arm.

6. It is important for you to scoop your dog's rear end so he feels secure. If you start by catching your dog by reaching over your dog's back with your left arm, his rear end and rear legs will dangle, making many dogs feel not very secure.

For Dogs That Are Vertical Jumpers (or Jump too Early)

It is important that a dog learn from a young age that discs always move from away from them and fly from low to high. Even eight-week-old puppies should learn to look for low to high, and the best way for very young puppies is to use a treat with your puppy sitting down perpendicular to you so you can move to your right.

1. Show the puppy the treat by placing it on the puppy's nose so he can smell it, then slowly move the treat to the ground. Then raise the treat up, saying "look," and reward the puppy with his head looking up with a

A dog catch over a hurdle.

"yes" and the treat. Once the puppy knows how to follow the treat, you can increase the lowering and raising speed of your treat hand. However, this exercise is not meant to be fast, just normal speed the dog can follow.

2. For older dogs, using a disc right side up is more effective. Start with the dog in the same perpendicular position, so he can run past you, but have the dog farther back.

3. Start off kneeling with your dog in a sitting position, and hold the disc in one vertical plane. The disc should start at the dog's nose (so he sees it), then lower it directly to the ground, saying "Fido, take it," while raising the disc up for him to take two feet higher than his nose. Remember, that the disc should be moved in one plane at a time, usually vertical first, then horizontal, then finally in both a vertical and horizontal plane.

4. Once he's good at this game both of you move to a standing position (stationary) and start the exercises over again.

5. When throwing, we typically want the dog to look up to catch, but learn to follow the flying disc from low to high so he catches the disc on the up flight, especially in distance throws as the dog has too much speed for running and catching while looking down.

Hanging Jumping Drill

This is one of my favorite jumping drills, which has successfully taught an un-natural jumper (who would jump in a stretch while dragging her back legs on the ground) to jump with ease and actually feel comfortable jumping and adjusting in mid-air.

1. Start with a hurdle close to a couch (see image), with the bar of the hurdle at the couch seat height.

2. If the dog has no problem jumping this height five times, move the hurdle back five to six inches at the same height, and start the exercise over. (The farthest distance for a nineteen-inch tall border collie who weighs thirty-five pounds is about five feet onto the couch.)

3. Once your dog can jump this distance, then you can place the hurdle back close to the couch and raise the bar up two inches at a time, still moving the hurdle back from the couch after every five successful jumps. This hanging jumping drill will teach your dog how to like the air and adjust their body by hanging. What you want is for your dog to shift his weight on his rear end just before he leaps and then effortlessly hang or pause in the air looking for the landing on the couch.

If your dog does not weigh too much, pick him up and make a game of gently jumping from your arms onto a bed. This exercise is the perfect test to see how your dog lands on the ground. With practice, your dog will be using his legs as shock absorbers, and while the game advances, you can even gently toss your dog onto the bed with a "ready, set, go." Remember that young dogs can jump up into your arms, up into a double-stacked crate, or even onto a bed very safely. It's the landing from the jumping down that dogs should not do until their growth plates close.

Learning to hang in mid-air by jumping over a hurdle to build confidence and rear end collection on a soft landing.

Stride Adjustment Tips

Many people think that for a dog, catching a disc while running and jumping is natural; however, many dogs have to be taught how to adjust their stride and shift their weight on their hindquarters just before they leap. So, having your dog practice catching a floating disc while jumping a hurdle can be an invaluable tool to help teach stride and shifting adjustments. If you understand skateboarding, it is just like shifting your weight on the back of the skateboard just before a jump. Shifting before a leap helps your dog control his leap, airtime, and landing while learning proper jumping technique.

▶ Keep your jump heights varied. This does two things: One, it keeps the dog from getting bored; and two, it keeps the dog alert and he usually become a more confident and smarter jumper.

▶ Vary your stride distance on the approach of the jump. Try using one and a half of your dog's stride lengths from the jump as your dog will have to shift back, rocking his hips back just before he lifts off. Adding half strides to full-length strides is an excellent training method for correcting stutter stepping, which can be exhibited in even experienced jumpers.

▶ If stutter stepping or refusing specific jumping tricks becomes an issue, then it's important to slow down and re-teach your dog better jumping judgment and help him re-gain confidence and stride adjustment. The best confidence builder is to go back to the basics and re-teach some of the fundamental easier jumping-over-the-body tricks. However, this time you are going to slow your dog down and re-teach him to jump from a sit, then a stand, then from a short run up, and finally from a farther away run up. This what I call going back to kindergarten. Do it for a few training sessions and quickly speed up back to your present more difficult drills.

▶ Sometimes you will also notice that your dog jumps late and pops up at the last moment or even drags his back legs while jumping. This usually happens with inexperienced dogs, or it could be a physical problem. This is a good time to get your dog checked out by a veterinarian.

▶ Any time your dog refuses to do a specific trick he normally has no problem doing, consider it to be a physical problem. Make a trip to the vet.

Two-Plane Floaters Over Hurdle

1. This is when you throw a disc in two flight planes over a jump so the disc is released up and out at the same time. Start by having the dog move to the disc thrown slightly off center of the jump bar. To accomplish this stand on the opposite side of the jump as your dog and float the disc up and out only two discs lengths from the bar. Slowly advance your throws by adding more disc lengths away from your dog's face while he still jumps over the hurdle. There is a limit on how far your dog can leap over the hurdle, hang, and catch the floating disc. A dog's liftoff to his landing can be an average of four- or five-times a dog's running stride distance. Don't push for too much distance—only push for safe, confident and controlled jumping.

2. As an advanced drill, you can start throwing in a more direct line where now the disc is moving toward the dog over the jump. The throw should never fly so far toward the dog that he catches the disc on the same side of the hurdle as he took off from on his jump starting position, but always catch on the landing side of the hurdle.

3. In order to turn your dog into a more versatile jumping disc dog that feels comfortable in the air during his mid-jump catching, you need to build his confidence with his body in mid-jump. This can be done by first building confidence at catching a disc, then at jumping and catching a disc, then jumping and catching a disc over a hurdle. This can be proofed through this exercise.

4. Start this drill with the dog on the left side of a hurdle with you on the right side. Stand perpendicular to your dog so your dog can pass by you.

5. Say, "Fido, go" while floating the disc in a vertical plane on the right side of the jump hurdle, but perpendicular to your dog.

6. Once your dog can catch this floater consistently, step two feet away and repeat the exercise. Continue moving to the right in two-feet increments with a vertical plane throw where the dog moves to the disc.

You can do the same exercise without the jump bar.

Two-Plane Jumping Drill with a Direct Throw Over Hurdle

This is the same concept as having the dog jump over the hurdle and take or catch a throw, but you're standing at least four to six feet away from the hurdle.

1. Throw directly at your dog while he jumps over the hurdle. This is challenging to say the least for both of you, but it builds the dog's confidence in jumping and catching, as he has to time his jump and catch.

2. Once your dog can catch a floater disc without knocking the bar over, you are ready for even more advanced jumping drills. Stand about six feet from the hurdle, turn your body slightly toward the hurdle, and throw the disc at a more direct line to the dog's running path. This is to teach the dog to jump and catch discs thrown in a more direct line to his face. This challenges him to catch the disc at different parts of the apex of the disc's flight. This throw should only be a floater, and your goal is to have the disc's flight apex be at the dog's jump height with the dog catching the disc as his rear legs just clear the bar. To do this, the dog will have to anticipate the throw's height, distance, and speed. The perfect exercise is where the dog glides effortlessly, catching the disc, jumping the hurdle, and landing with a solid collection.

A direct throw over the hurdle.

One plane (vertical).

Two planes (vertical and horizontal).

Touch Desensitization While Jumping

This is a fun exercise if your dog likes to tug on the disc or a tug rope.

1. Standing perpendicular to your dog, hold the disc upside down in your right hand at 6 o'clock with your fingers on top and your thumb under the disc.

2. Squat down with your left leg slightly forward, placing two-thirds of your weight on your back right leg.

3. Bend your elbow only halfway, extending the disc in front of your right shoulder.

4. While the dog is in mid-jump, let him take the disc gently out of your right hand. Meanwhile, touch him on the belly with the palm of your left hand.

5. One exercise is to let the dog take the disc from you and only touch his belly momentarily— gently holding him in the air as he takes the disc from you. However, your ultimate goal is to touch your dog's belly and hold the dog in the air for one or two seconds, with you still holding onto the disc with your right hand. This is where the tug comes in, as the dog will not take the disc from you but gently bite and tug on the disc, while you momentarily hold him up in the air. Then you'll finally gently lower him down.

6. This exercise will teach your dog to feel comfortable and realize he can pause in the air. It helps your dog get used to you touching his body, and teaches him to pause, hang in the air, and feel comfortable.

Touch desensitization while jumping.

Dismount from Dog Catch

As a dog disc athlete, these dogs do something that no other dog sport requires, which is to flip in mid-air while catching a disc and also vault off your body (see the next two chapters in this section). So, here is a trade secret of mine that I use with all of my young dogs to make sure they know how to look for the ground and control their flipping rotation. This dismount teaches your dog to roll out of your arms and look for the ground while you place them on the ground gently.

A dismount from a dog catch or holding the dog so the dog learns to roll and find the ground.

1. Place the dog in your arms upside down, like holding a baby, belly up. Once the dog is calm, roll the dog out of your arms while lowering your body to the ground safely.

2. Set the dog down gently. What this does is teach the dog to upright himself like a cat, and that if he is in an awkward position, like half upside down, he knows he can control his body, roll or turn, look for the ground, and place his feet down.

3. If your dog is uncomfortable in this position then start by sitting on the ground and roll him upright.

Flipping

Your dog doesn't need to be able to flip to enjoy catching a flying disc; however, if you are interested in some serious fun or you want to compete, flipping is definitely a crowd-pleaser.

THE HORIZONTAL OR HELICOPTER FLIP

In canine disc, many dogs that bound and bounce up vertically and can be taught to bounce up and turn around (flip) like a helicopter. This helicopter flip is one of the safest types of flips you can teach your dog since he never loses sight of the horizon (the ground).

1. Stand directly in front of your dog and hold a disc vertically at about 1 o'clock, with your dog at 12 o'clock.

2. With your left leg in front of your body, lean in and teach your dog to take the disc at three feet up and three feet out from the center of his back to your right.

3. Once your dog can take the disc at this height, then, while the dog is in mid-jump, still holding the disc at 1 o'clock, drop the disc's outside edge where your hand is holding it to 3 o'clock. However, leave the opposite side of the disc in the same place. This is called the drop take.

4. This drop take from a flip will help develop your dog's flip into a bigger catching radius. Once your dog can take the drop from a flip, start with a short throw that's almost a stalled disc rotating in place, but move the disc from 1 o'clock to 2 o'clock, and then finally throw the disc at the 3 o'clock position. Some dogs need to slowly transition from a take drop to a take position with a small quarter turn on the disc, stalling the disc's spin in one spot, on a barely released disc, before you can throw the disc at 3 o'clock.

5. The best way to measure how high your dog should need the disc thrown is to imagine if your dog stood in front of you and stood straight up. How tall is his mouth in

A flip.

height in a stand tall? Now, imagine if your dog, while standing, could rotate his body to 3 o'clock, still touching the ground with his feet. Where would his mouth be? This is the minimum height you need to throw the disc, preferably throwing the disc a little flatter at 1 to 3 o'clock. Remember that the best rule of thumb is three feet up and three feet out from your dog's butt is where you need to throw a flatter disc to get the full rotation and safe flipping motion.

6. After landing, you want your dog to turn and face you for another flip. The best way to teach this is to have your dog do a flip. Then, call his name and have him do a direct, easy, straight-mouth catch. This helps the dog complete his flipping rotation and land looking at you after each flip. This also helps take the impact out of the landing so the dog continues to move out of his flip to look at you.

Flipping sequence.

Now the dog is turned in mid-air to look for the ground.

Other Types of Flips

One of the mistakes many people make when wanting to flip their dog is to teach them by throwing a vertical disc directly over their dogs' head at 12 o'clock. This allows the dog to choose if he wants to fly left or right and also creates more of a cartwheel flip. From my twenty-four years of experience, cartwheel flips tend to overload the front end of a dog and puts undo stress on his wrists, elbow, shoulders and neck. When the dog lands directly on his front or directly on his rear it's called overloading. Many dog agility organizations have even modified their obstacles heights and angles to minimize overloading a competition dog's front end. With the proper time, patience, and instruction, any disc dog can learn to flip safely in an up-and-around motion. My drop-take technique can change just about any dog's flipping style and increase his flipping catching radius.

Stretch and Full Stretch Jump

This is where dog reaches out in front of his body with the legs stretched. If a dog is using a full stretch, his hind legs are extended horizontal to the ground.

Tuck and Full Tuck Jump

The wrists are folded under the dog's chest with his hind legs bent, folded tight, under his knees.

Hip Turn or Kick to the Side Jump

This is what you normally see Aussies do when they jump. This is a mid-air adjustment and can be caused by the dog anticipating a turn ahead, or maybe from a powerful hind as their rear pushes too hard. This can happen when performing an over-the-body jump in free-style flying disc when a dog is reaching to one side for a disc. The dog will collect and rotate his hips the same direction as he reaches out and stretches, catching the disc.

Hoover Jumping (Hang Time)

Many dogs with perfect structure, like a Whippet, do this naturally with such grace. However, you can develop this type of hang time with nearly any dog through jumping hanging drills onto a couch or a bed mattress. See page 110.

Front Flip

- ▶ Wait until your dog is twelve months or older before training for flips.
- ▶ You can change a dog's flipping style to become more round like a helicopter, up and around, by throwing a disc to him the way he likes it (his flipping sweet spot), and then throw a disc where you want him to go. The dog may miss a few, but if you rotate back and forth from one flip he knows and one you want him to learn, he will eventually learn the second type. This is what I call challenging the dog's catching radius on flips.

- ▶ Many dogs flip into their owners because the disc is too close to the owner's body. Flipping toward you can definitely be a safe flipping style and has its advantages when you want to flip and catch your dog. But if you do not teach your dog to flip up and land like a helicopter, then you will limit what types of flips your dog can do.
- ▶ Do not ever attempt to turn your dog in mid-flip while the disc is in your dog's mouth. The dog must build up enough confidence to rotate on his own.

▶ Personally, I never surprise my dog in the learning phase of catching a disc, especially in a flip to a dog catch. You will be more successful in teaching a flip if you stand directly in front of your dog and step in and have him take a disc slightly to the side, same side as your throwing hand. This way your dog is comfortable with the leaping height, angle, rotation, and landing. With this method, you can also change your dog's flip and catching radius. Many people tell me that their dog can only do a cartwheel and will not jump high enough. Well if you deliver the disc at a vertical angle directly over the dog's head at 12 o'clock, the dog cannot jump very high and can only do a cartwheel, which usually makes the dog land on his front end, while his butt is above his head and his rear legs swing around. This type of flip will limit your dog's catching radius and can eventually create strain at the dog's weakest point on his body, the T-13 vertebrae. This is why I do not teach cartwheel flips. A dog that is not comfortable flipping is 99 percent of the time a cartwheel-flipping dog.

- The second flip I do not personally like is the full flip. This is where the dog flips directly end over end, doing a full 360 degrees in the air. Many shorter backed dogs can do this successfully, but it is a complete vertical jump while rotating upside down, and it can be difficult for a dog to recover and roll out of a misjudged flip as his back is completely to the ground at some point.
- Remember that any dog sport can be done safely. Remember also that your dog trusts you and if he refuses a trick, find out why before continuing. Sometimes the dog is telling you he does not have enough confidence to do that, or not enough experience to control his body. Or perhaps there is something physical that is creating an issue for your dog. Many owners assume their dogs are just being stubborn, when usually, the dog is communicating that he doesn't know how to do what you're asking.
- When teaching a flip, remember that there are two arches of the disc's flying trajectory: one is a vertical arch from you to the dog, which should be like the first arch on a McDonald's "M"; and the second is from 12 to 3 o'clock, where 12 o'clock starts on your head height and 3 o'clock is at your shoulder height. But this clock is out away from you as the dog's butt is at 6 o'clock.
- Any straight line throw directly over the dog's head, whether it is a vertical or flat throw, will generate a full flip or vertical cartwheel, which creates vertical landings, or swing landings, that overload your dog's front end, which I do not recommend.
- You can change and modify your dog's flipping style, but teach him to flip from a sit, or even a sit between your legs, which is what I call a through flip. Start with a vertical take from a sit where your dog is between your legs facing the same direction you are and then gradually stand up.
- Once your dog starts flipping, toss a disc to his face as a reward straight catch. This will teach your dog to flip, land, and finish his turn all the way around to you so he is ready for anything else.
- Remember that when teaching forward jumping drills to your dog, it is important when your dog is running to have him come from a straight line of at least two full body strides before the jump and after the jump. Then, moving out of the landing is another crucial part of jumping, which helps cushion the impact of the dog's weight during the landing. Dogs with advanced jumping skills can adjust their bodies in mid-air. So, teach your dog to jump and run straight out after landing. As a dog gets more advanced, you can have him jump, flip or vault, and turn and move out of a cushioned landing. Landings that end in a hard stop or a complete vertical jump followed by a vertical landing, whether the dog lands on four feet or vertically on two rear legs, is extremely hard on the dog's joints and mid back. Whether a dog is jumping over your body, a hurdle, or off your body, it is important to train your dog with jumping drills so he is comfortable with all of the jumping styles and speeds required. The most important lesson your dog must learn is that he can control his own body in mid-air and landings.

Vaulting

A vault by definition is where a dog touches a person's body part, pushing off it, to get a thrown disc. The most successful vaults to teach are the ones where the dog can see the disc in plain sight before and during the leap up to vault off your body. With my first border collie, Cody, for the first six months of his life we taught him not to jump up on people or touch people. Boy, were we sorry when I wanted to teach him how to vault off me. So, here is a simple method I created to help new dogs learn how to touch and push off a person's body for vaulting.

1. One of the easiest ways to teach a dog to vault is teach him the word "touch" by you kneeling on the ground, bending your leg to his side. In the learning stage, a bent leg means "vault" and an extended leg means "jump over."

2. Start with your dog on your left side and kneel down, bending your left knee. Touch your left knee to a wall. This creates a direct path for your dog.

3. Ask your dog to touch your bent leg by patting your leg. You first want him to touch your leg with his front paws, and then you extend your right hand holding a disc as far as your arm can reach away from your dog.

4. Now, the dog will usually try to climb up and get the disc. When he does this, capture it and then touch and push your leg by saying "touch." Now, if he tries to jump, withhold the disc and do not let him have it and try again. You can even place his front legs on your leg and then lift his butt up and place his back feet on your leg and say "touch."

5. Another way to teach your dog to vault is for you to get on all fours, teaching them the word "table" or the phrase "load up," luring them with food at first to do a back stall.

6. Sometimes you will need a target treat-stick to guide your dog on your back or you will need another person to lure the dog on your back.

7. Once your dog is on your back and he can load up on command for a back stall, add a disc and extend your hand out to your right with a backhand floater throw and float the disc up about two feet while saying "touch." Sometimes this is the fastest way to teach your dog to "touch" as you are capturing the dog leaping off your back going for the disc and pairing it with the "touch" command.

8. A third method of teaching vaulting is to kneel on all fours, with your left side to your dog, and have a second person stand by your feet. This person will reach out and hold the disc to your right side with the dog on your left side. Have the second person tap your back with her left hand and say "touch."

Teaching vaulting and the word "touch."

Vaulting Gallery

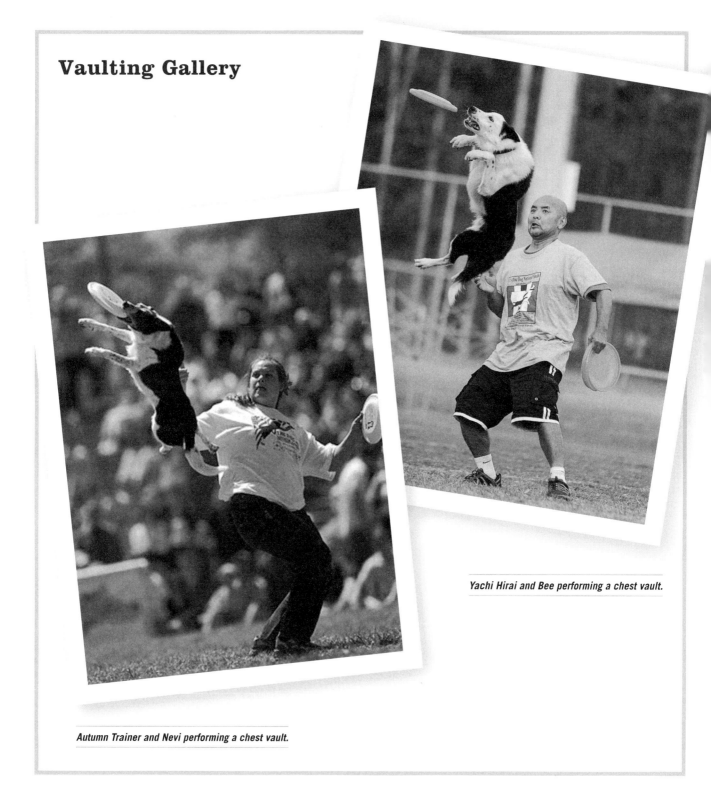

Yachi Hirai and Bee performing a chest vault.

Autumn Trainer and Nevi performing a chest vault.

Shaun Hirai and Shack performing a foot fault and chest vault to a dog catch.

Melissa and Asah performing a back vault from right to left.

*Melissa and Ariel Asah, 1997
Canine Disc World Champions.*

Veronika Urbaskova from the Czech Republic.

Pam Martin and Pilot performing a foot vault from the ground.

Sabine (Bruns) Wolff and Y performing a leg vault.

Melissa and Glory performing a leg vault.

*Chuck and Bling Bling,
World Champions.*

▶ If you're serious about competing, I recommend that you consider purchasing a vaulting vest. It should not be too thin as it will bunch up on your body and limit your movement, and it should not be too slick or it could become slippery under your shirt. Or, consider wearing two t-shirts or a sweatshirt. Just be careful when wearing sweatshirts with pockets or any pants with pockets. Your dog could get his foot or toes caught in them.

▶ Do not vault your dog until he is at least twelve to eighteen months old or you have confirmed through X-rays that your dog's large growth plates are closed.

▶ Once your dog knows how to vault, you do not need to repeat this in your daily or even weekly training. I usually recommend vaulting one session or training routine every other week. In the off-season my dogs typically do not vault at all.

▶ People always ask how high is too high for a vaulting dog. My rule of thumb is that if I am standing up then the throw is delivered so the dog is vaulting on a more horizontal trajectory. So, out is better than up. This way, the dog can see what body part to push off of, how high to push, and how far to push off your body.

▶ Make sure you master the straight vaulting style, where your dog starts on one side of your body, vaults off, and then lands on the other side of your body, a passing vault. You can vary the grips, releases, and body stances before trying any reverse vaulting motions. It is more difficult to teach a dog to bank off your body and should be taught after the basic move is learned.

Lucka Schonova from the Czech Republic.

Flexibility Training

Stretching and flexibility are extremely important for dogs in dog sports and are the keys for a long, healthy toss & fetch career for your dog, whether he's competing or just playing at the park. Here are just a few types of stretching exercises. Check with your veterinarian, veterinarian chiropractor, or certified canine massage therapist to confirm you are performing these stretches properly.

When you stretch, extend, or flex a joint, muscle, or limb hold gently for thirty seconds, release, and repeat three times for thirty seconds each. Don't forget to do both sides equally. If your dog doesn't like any of the stretches, don't force them. Simply release and try again, gently. Note: The images on the next three pages feature Monami Konishi, DVM, Animal Chiropractor.

Shoulder front stretch: make sure you support the elbow and stretch straight forward with an ever-so-slight rotation in toward the dog's chest.

Flex wrist: Checking your dog's wrist flexibility is important, as jumping dogs tend to tighten their forearm muscles between their wrist and elbow, which ultimately tightens their inner and outer shoulder muscles. It is imperative to relax these muscles. This stretch can be done with the dog lying on his side.

Nose side to side: You can stand or sit for this stretch and so can your dog. Stand or sit on one side of the dog and cup his nose and mouth in your hand, supporting his head. Stretch his nose toward his butt on one side, and repeat three times, holding each stretch for thirty seconds and then repeat on the other side.

Nose up and down: This is best if your dog is sitting (with you on one side of him) and using one hand cupping their lower mouth. Place your other hand on the back of his neck for support. Your goal is to slowly stretch your dog's nose to the sky. Then, place one hand on the back of your dog's neck for support and gently place your other hand on top of your dog's nose, gently stretching his nose down, straight down. Your goal is to stretch their nose in between their knees.

Bend knee and hock together: Kneeling on your dog's left side, reach under his belly with your left hand and support the right knee. Then with your right hand, reach around your dog's butt and pick up your dog's same right hock. Keeping close to the dog's body, lift the hock toward their same right knee.

Reverse between the legs: Stand with your dog standing between your legs, with the dog facing backward. Reach down, crossing your arms so you're reaching the dog's opposite knees. Lift his knees up toward your shoulders, but do not lift directly to the sky as this can lead to overloading your dog's front end. This is a good stretch if a dog has a hip that is tipped up too much.

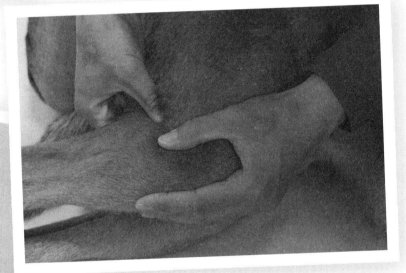

Hamstring stretch: With all of the power leaping a disc dog does, his hamstrings tend to get tight. So, here is how to check your dog's hamstring and stretch it. Kneel down with your dog facing the same direction as you. Pick up his hock and bring it in close to his same side of their body. Now, supporting his same knee, gently and slowly lift the hock up and forward toward his shoulder with his toes pointed to the sky. The goal is to very slowly stretch this hamstring muscle, and hopefully your dog's toe can lift higher than the tip of his shoulder blade.

Throwing the Disc

There are many different types of throws used in canine disc sports, but when beginning, you only need to remember a few. A successful throw must have enough spin on it so that it hovers or floats and doesn't just drop to the ground.

FLOATER THROW

This throw is the most versatile throw for freestyle. It is used for overs, flips, vaults, multiples, and some closer-in zigzags or arounds. A floater is a clockwise spin and can be thrown flat or with a little angle. It can be thrown vertically like an elevator or up and out. (To get a floater to go up and out, have your hand finish facing out about your nose height away from your face. It is just like shooting a basketball.)

1. Start with the backhand grip (page 59).

2. Shake your hand like you have a pair of rolling dice in your hand and place the disc inside your bent fingers.

3. Place your thumb on top of the disc (actually on the ridges of the disc) with your first finger on the outside rim of the disc.

4. Bend your first finger at the first knuckle, wrapping it around the bottom of the disc.

Your little finger and ring finger are wrapped tight on the inside rim of the disc with some pressure.

5. The next important pressure point is between your wrapped first finger, wrapped on the bottom of the disc rim, and your thumb. Now, this is the backhand floater grip.

6. For right-handed throwers place your left leg slightly in front of your right for your stance position and face your throwing target. The motion is mostly from your elbow to your wrist.

7. To throw a floater straight up, you only need to swing your arm down from your elbow, then up toward your face, snapping mostly with your wrist. Right before you release the disc, change your grip by releasing your fingers while lifting the disc straight up. All of your fingers should be pointing up and together at the end of this throw.

8. A trick of getting the floater to fly vertically straight up is to not only point your fingers to the sky, but just after the release, physically touch your fingers to your nose.

This helps you learn to lift the disc vertically on the release. Trust me it really does.

9. Another secret is to place your left hand vertically in the crease of your right elbow and use your left hand as a stopper. This will also make you snap the disc lifting it straight up.

What floaters are used for!

Try sitting in chair or on the ground with your legs folded and practice throwing the floater vertically to yourself. Then practice catching the disc in the backhand grip and throwing it again. This is a muscle-memory motor skill of throwing and catching with the same hand using the same grip. Boy, it works like a charm.

Two-Handed Floater

A two-handed floater is where you spin the disc in a vertical and or horizontal flight pattern with both hands. The throwing stance if really flexible on this throw as the throw requires more motion from your elbows to your fingers.

1. Start by holding the disc's top plate to the sky. Then place the disc between both your hands, where your fingers are facing the sky and the disc is being held between our middle knuckles at 9 o'clock and 3 o'clock.

2. Rotate your right hand to 6 o'clock (which is in front of your face) with your left hand at 12 o'clock (the farthest away from your face).

The two-handed floater.

3. When you rotate the disc your fingers will naturally change from the middle of your knuckles to more of the tips of your fingers, with your thumb also touching the disc.

4. Start with your elbows near your body and begin the upward motion from your elbows. With equal snap and spin on the disc lift your elbows up and snap the disc upward.

5. At the end of the snap, your right hand should finish like you are shooting a basketball, and your left hand will be bent at the wrist and touching your left shoulder.

6. This throw can be down in two planes (vertical and horizontal) in an up-and-out throw, too. However, to get the disc to go more horizontal than vertical, you must stop your left hand when snapping from 12 o'clock, and stopping at 9 o'clock. So, your right hand still snaps as if it is dunking a basketball, but the left hand stops with half the spin. (Your right hand has to push twice as much as the left.) An easy way to understand this is to hold the disc at 9 and 3 again, and just push and roll the disc with your right hand, not moving your left hand.

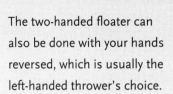

TRAINER'S TIP

The two-handed floater can also be done with your hands reversed, which is usually the left-handed thrower's choice. This throw will spin clockwise.

A two-handed, upside down push floater.

An easy way to throw the disc sidearm and learn to snap your wrists is to place another disc under your right elbow and wedge it between your elbow and body side during the throwing motion. Do not drop the wedged disc while throwing.

Sidearm Throw (Forearm)

1. Position your body with your left leg facing your throwing field and your right leg hip-distance apart and slightly behind your front leg.

2. Shift two-thirds of your body weight on your back right leg and lower your right shoulder.

3. Start by making a peace sign with your right hand, now open your thumb and extend it all the way.

4. Place the disc between your thumb and two fingers. Your thumb is on the high side of the disc, at 12 o'clock, with the bottom plate facing your right knee. Your middle finger is on the inside of the rim facing your throwing field.

5. This throw is all in the wrist and must be snapped at a complete vertical angle. The best way to learn this throw is to shift your weight so much on your back right leg that you can bend over to your right touching the low side of the disc (the 6 o'clock side of the disc) to the ground. Snap your wrist forward vertically pointing your fingers toward your throwing field.

6. Adding a different release to the sidearm throw is to lift your left leg and throw underneath your left leg. This does two things: It makes you release at the correct vertical angle by lowering your right shoulder, and it makes you use just your wrist during the throw.

The sidearm throw.

Upside Down, Left to Right

1. Using the sidearm grip, hold the disc upside down on your left side.

2. Stagger your legs with your left leg in front of your right.

3. Drop your left shoulder, like a backhand tennis swing, and snap the disc across your body from the left to the right. It's as easy as a snap of the wrist. Your hand is on the high side of the disc with the opposite side angled down.

The hammer.

Hammer, Upside Down

1. Start with the sidearm throw.

2. Shift two-thirds of your weight on your back right leg with your left leg slightly in front of your right hip.

3. Now rock forward shifting your weight onto your left front leg, drop your left shoulder lower than your right.

4. Touch the top plate to your right ear, leaning on your left leg and snap the disc forward.

5. This throw is almost all snap from your elbow to your wrist. As you get more proficient, you do not have to bend over so much, and you won't have to touch your disc's top plate to your ear.

Wrist Flip

1. Hold the disc in your right hand using the backhand grip. Loosen your grip.

2. Now, hold the disc with both hands like reading a book, with your left hand at 9 o'clock and your right hand at 3.

3. Spin the disc with your left hand end over end so it ends up upside down in your right hand.

4. Place your thumb firmly against the inside rim. Let go with your left hand.

5. Stand with your left leg slightly in front of your right leg. Shift two-thirds of your weight on your left front leg and drop your left shoulder.

6. For new throwers, rotate the disc back clockwise and place the disc (bottom plate) on top of your right wrist and forearm. Release the disc at a somewhat of a vertical angle with the outside of the disc lower that your grip.

7. Your grip is now at the top of the disc. Snap the disc forward. Even though there is some movement with the elbow, this throw is mostly all wrist snapping forward toward your field.

The wrist flip.

Practicing the wrist flip from a kneeling position.

Staker Throw

1. Stand with your chest facing forward and your left leg facing forward slightly in front of your right.

2. Hold the disc upside down in your non-throwing hand and grab the disc with your other hand at 6 o'clock. Place your thumb on the inside rim of the disc facing 7 o'clock. Then place your first finger on the top plate (facing the ground at this point), and wedge the outer rim of the disc between your first and second fingers.

3. Now, flip the disc over toward your face so your hand is now at 12 o'clock, closest to your throwing field, and the opposite side of the disc is closest to your face just below your chin.

4. Rotate the disc all the way around the clock, counterclockwise, to 6 o'clock. The disc will turn around and actually rotate over your right throwing arm.

5. The throwing motion is a snap from the wrist.

6. The trick to this throw is release it at a slightly higher angle and end your throwing motion with your thumb pointing toward your throwing field. The disc should be released at somewhat of a vertical angle, but it will rotate to a flat position as it spins clockwise.

The staker throw.

Staker Push Throw

1. This throw is the same as a staker with the exception that all of your fingers, except your pinky, are on top of the disc's top plate. The little finger is on the side of the outer rim.

2. Your stance is the same but you are now throwing to your right instead of directly in front of you.

3. The motion is also different. Now you will go out to your right at 3 o'clock and stretch your arm out completely and circle your arm from 3 o'clock to 12 o'clock (your head height) and then to 6 o'clock, and then finally, back to 3 o'clock for the release. So, you have done a 360-degree circle with your arm snapping your wrist to your right and pointing your thumb toward your target. The disc flight pattern should be released at somewhat of a vertical angle, but it will rotate to a flat position as it spins clockwise.

The staker push.

Thumber Throw

1. This throw has the same grip as the staker, but the throwing motion is to reach back with your right arm as if you are throwing a baseball, with your left leg slightly in front of your right leg.

2. The disc's bottom is facing your right ear and your grip is at 6 o'clock, the low side of the disc.

3. With your right arm now bent at the elbow, start the throwing motion, leading with your elbow first and then snap your wrist with a vertical angle on the disc. The nose of the disc, two to three inches from your thumb grip, is at 9 o'clock at this point—facing the throwing field.

4. The exact release should be vertical and with a snap forward. Even though you're using some arm motion, this throw could be done with almost all wrist snap. The disc should have a small arch to its flight and land flat as it rotates counterclockwise.

The staker.

The upside-down backhand.

Upside-down Backhand

1. Stand with your left leg in front of your right leg, hip distance apart.

2. Hold the disc in both of hands right side up at 9 and 3 o'clock.

3. Remove your left hand and rotate the disc, bending your elbow so the disc is coiled up onto your right shoulder. At this point your hand is now at 12 o'clock.

4. Shift two-thirds of your weight onto your back right leg and uncoil your wrist, snapping it to the sky.

5. At the release point, your hand will finish at 9 o'clock. The disc flight pattern should be up like a rainbow, and the disc should land spinning counterclockwise to a flat position.

Many of different releases and grips should be practiced from not only the normal standing position, but also from a kneeling, sitting, and lying down position. Once you start practicing in freestyle flying disc you will find that training from different awkward positions will be come invaluable.

Dog Grip Drill 1: Catching Multiple Discs While Sitting

1. Concentrate on keeping the dog stationary in a sit.

2. Start with five discs fanned out at right angles, pinching the discs tightly closed with your left hand. (The more vertical the discs are in your hand, the faster you can throw the discs.)

The underside of the pinched discs and your grip.

3. Take the discs from the bottom of the stack and arch each throw like a one-sided McDonald's "M."

4. The discs should fall into your dog's mouth.

5. Change your angle of the disc to flat and then reverse the angle of the disc. Also, vary your speed and trajectory to get your dog used to different situations. Try each multiple upside down in the same three angles, right, then straight, then left. It is also another challenge if you throw the multiples side to side.

Airen learning stationary multiples.

TRAINER'S TIP

The two-handed throws provide more great bite work, as each two-handed has a different spinning direction. Try throwing the two-handed throws with the discs upside down. Can your dog bite down and grip both clockwise and counterclockwise throws, right side up and upside down?

Glory proofing her multiples on a stationary object.

Improving Your Throwing Skills

The way to improve your accuracy and consistency is to throw . . . a lot. By practicing different grips and releases with another person or into a large hanging net, through a tire, or into a drawn box on the wall, you will quickly gain confidence with the variety of throws presented in this book.

TARGETING DRILLS

1. Use chalk or tape to draw two boxes on the wall at your dog's height at his head. The first box should be twelve to eighteen inches square and have a large X in the middle. The second box should measure as if your dog was standing straight up on his hind legs and tipped over sideways to two o'clock. You can also use a dog agility tire or tire swing if you have one.

2. Start with the kneeling multiple throws, first your right angle, then your center, then your left angle, and then back and forth multiples.

3. Now, stand up and do the same exercises and angles in the standing box.

4. The next challenge for you to throw a floater in a vertical plane to yourself, catching the disc in the correct grip, and then throwing a floater and hitting the center of the box. This exercise is good practice for flips and vaults.

5. Practice throwing all of your different angles in the floater, right, left, and then center.

Back view of angled target practice.

Center angle practice.

Angled practice.

Upside-down drill.

Motor Skill Drill

When considering competition, one of the most valuable drills is to stand in front of a mirror and call out the names of the throws and practice the different grips, stance positions, and motions.

1. Call out to yourself the name of each grip and get in that throwing starting stance position. If you are training with a group of friends, then the most experienced person calls out the names and everyone has to mimic each grip, stance, and motion when called out.

2. Don't forget to change your grip and your stance on each throw called out, not just the grip. This is a fun game and anyone practicing this learns quickly.

Backhand

Behind-the-back backhand.

Sidearm

Hammer

Between-the legs floater.

Upside-down throw.

TRAINER'S TIP

Another advanced drill is to throw a floater up, and while the disc is in mid-air, grab it in a different grip and then move into a new stance for a different throw.

Staker

Wind Drills

1. Set up four cones set in a square, with each twenty yards apart.

2. Throw ten to twenty discs from one side of the square to the other side.

3. Pick up the discs and throw them to the other side until you have completed all four sides of the square. This allows you to throw in all the basic wind conditions: downwind, cross wind from the right, into the wind, and cross wind from the left. As you get proficient, your discs will land closer and closer together near your target.

Cloverleaf Freestyle Throwing

1. Set out three cones in a cloverleaf pattern, each cone thirty yards apart, and practice all of your throwing drills outside on a large playing field.

2. Throw all five discs to the first one, run and pick them up, then do a set of multiples at that station, and then throw a different grip or release to the second cone station.

3. Run and pick the discs, and then throw a zigzag at the third cone station.

4. Pick up all your discs and run back past a finishing line. You can time yourself or use your own segments of your routine to practice field presentation and field movement.

Ready to Compete?

Most pet owners reading this book will be perfectly happy learning the basics of disc dog and perhaps a few of the advanced techniques. But some of you are going to catch the bug in a big way and will want to compete. Here are the basics for getting ready to enter a competition with your dog, as well as what I've learned during my years of competition and teaching others to compete.

Competition Rules

Toss & Fetch competition is simply a test of your dog's retrieval skills. The field is thirty yards wide by sixty yards long, with out of bounds on the left and right and a starting line. You have ninety seconds for your dog to catch as many discs as possible, to reach the maximum score of 22.5 points. The rules were established so big, little, fast, and small dogs can all compete equally toward a perfect score.

The scores are 1, 2, 3, and 4 points allowed per throw (in the 10, 20, 30, 40 yard zones) with an additional 1/2 point for a mid-air catch. So, the highest five throws count toward your maximum total score of 22.5.

TOSS & FETCH FORMAT (USDDN WORLD FINALS SERIES)

▶ One dog, one disc, one player allowed on the field

▶ 90-second format

▶ Time starts when the dog crosses the line

▶ Unlimited throwing attempts

▶ Best of five highest scores count

▶ Can score up to 22.5 points per round

▶ A ground catch with any one foot on the ground during the catch is: 10 yards = 1pt, 20 yards = 2 pts, 30 yards = 3 pts, 40 yards = 4 pts

▶ A mid-air catch with all four feet clearly in the air during the catch is:
10 yards = 1pt, 20 yards = 2 pts,
30 yards = 3 pts, 40 yards = 4 pts

▶ Out of bounds is left and right sidelines

▶ No out-of-bounds forward

▶ A dog scores where the dog lands with the trailing foot closest to the throwing line

▶ The field of play minimum size is thirty yards wide by sixty yards long

▶ A player can exchange a disc by giving the foul/timer judge an extra disc

Field Diagrams

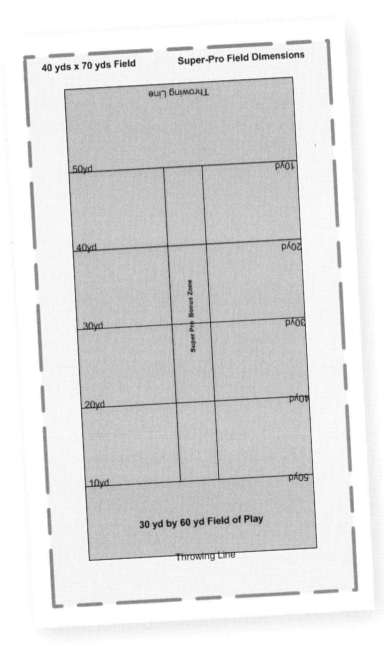

40 yds x 70 yds Field   Super-Pro Field Dimensions

Throwing Line

50yd   10yd

40yd   20yd

Super-Pro Bonus Zone

30yd   30yd

20yd   40yd

10yd   50yd

30 yd by 60 yd Field of Play

Throwing Line

Freestyle Format

▶ One dog, up to ten discs, one player is allowed on the field during time

▶ Two-minute format

▶ Scoring starts when the music starts and execution starts on the first throw

▶ Scoring is based on four elements: canine, up to 10 points; player, up to 10 points; team, up to 10 points; execution, up to 10 points

▶ Each element has sub-elements broken down into 2.5 scores totaling up to 10 points for that individual element

▶ The Freestyle total of 40 points in each round is multiplied by 1.5 for a total of 60 points

▶ If only one round of freestyle is performed, then the freestyle total of 40 points is multiplied by 3 points

▶ To get an over-all champion, the freestyle rounds are added to one Toss & Fetch round

▶ No out of bounds

▶ The field of play is, at a minimum, 30 yards wide by 60 yards long

For a full set of freestyle rules visit www. usddn.com (US Disc Dog Nationals USDDN - International Steering Committee).

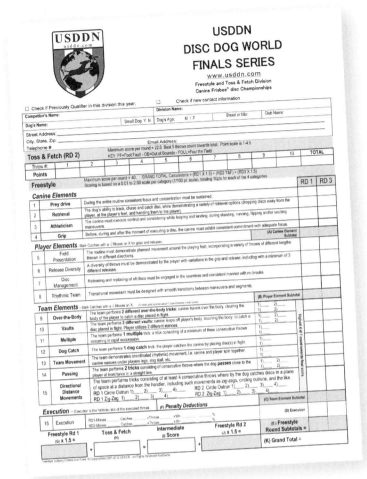

2013 USDDN Freestyle scoresheet

Serious Dog Disc Competition Considerations

▶ Before competing in freestyle flying disc competitions, your dog must be able to take a disc while sitting, standing, and running at different distances. Having your dog take a disc sounds simple, but it is not always, as many pet owners have taught their dogs not to take anything from their hands. For dog sports training, this is a mistake.

▶ Your dog must be proficient in many individual skills including toss & fetch, multiples, vaults, and/or flips. Once your dog has mastered four out of the seven team elements, then you can start making up a routine for your dog. However, remember that each skill needs to be proficient before chaining them into a segment.

▶ It is important to master the backhand throw and floater before competing in freestyle. So, I recommend practicing and competing in toss & fetch competitions for one year before competing in freestyle. In your second year, you should start practicing and training your dog in freestyle. At that time you can consider competing in an intermediate freestyle division.

▶ As a competitor, it is important to identify you and your dog's strengths and create your routine around them. Don't be something that you or your dog are not good at.

▶ When developing a routine for your dog, do not force him to perform maneuvers he is not comfortable with—especially if your dog does not have good structure for dog sports. Work with your own dog's abilities and currently trained skills.

▶ Training and at a local club gathering is always recommended for competition exposure for you and your dog.

▶ If you are serious about competing, it is best to have a training area at home, indoors and outdoors. Even if they are both small areas, you can do many of the conditioning exercises in a large room in your house or basement. In my basement I have a fifteen by twenty-four foot training room with padded professional Astro turf. However, you do not need professional turf, but a thick carpet with think padding. Even better, you can purchase interlocking two-foot squares of rubber matting. This is perfect for training indoors.

In the training room.

▶ The best rule of thumb is to make sure that your dog is physically fit and at his optimum body weight thirty days before the contest. Then make sure that you identify how your dog will best peak. If that means your dog is like my world-champion dog, Ariel Asah, your routine must be completely set one month before the tournament and then five times a week you practice your routine. Train like you will be competing, with freestyle first, then toss & fetch, and then freestyle again in one day. Make sure you have enough time so your dog can rest between each round.

▶ A good rule of thumb when training is to rest your dog double or triple the time you spend on the routine segment before working on the next one.

- Hydration is the key for a healthy body, so make sure you're hydrating your dog one week before a tournament and one week after. That means giving your dog water with some can food in it or one-half cup of dry nugget food in a one gallon jug of cool water. Shake it up and give it to him to drink during workouts. Make sure that nugget dry food does not swell in the gallon jug (just look for the smallest kibble possible), or better yet, get a dog sports electrolyte replacement, such as Rebound.

- Make sure your dog is within its ideal body weight for its breed. Any dog that is overweight can lose weight by starting a low-impact exercise program like walking and swimming. Most importantly, your dog must be on the appropriate weight-management diet to lose weight. If you just lower the amount of food your dog eats, that can work, but then your dog may not be receiving the correct amount of vitamins, nutrients, meat protein, fat, and fiber. Consult your veterinarian on which foods are right for your dog during his weight-loss period.

- Mental preparedness is both for you and your dog. The quickest way to get over your competition jitterbugs is to do fun demonstrations for your local club or a humane society. Performing for fun in no-pressure demonstrations will also help your dog get used to crowds and the cheering.

- Warm-ups and cool-downs are very important, so make sure that you walk you dog for at least twenty minutes before and after exercise to make sure your dog's muscles don't bind up and tighten.

- Having too few discs during a freestyle can hurt you and having too many and not using them all is just as bad. Disc management is about how you handle and hold discs in your hand and how you pick up and manage your tricks throughout your routine. It is important that a competitor varies how many discs are in each set and how smoothly and seamlessly a competitor picks up and replaces her discs.

- In the release diversity element of the judging, competitors need to perform a minimum of three different grips with different releases, and even though competitors receive scores for attempting difficult throws, the throws are judged on their quality. So a person who only throws backhands will not score higher than one who attempts more difficult throws; however, a competitor who throws difficult throws of poor quality will be judge accordingly. I recommend that competitors do not throw or perform any trick or grip or release that has not been 90-percent accurate before competition.

Team Movement or Freestyle Dancing

These moves are for the pre-routine and transitions between individual tricks and between tricks and segments. Several of the pre-routine tricks should be taught on a bucket. This helps your dog understand you want him to be stationary when you perform them.

Marni Brown and Cozmoe performing unique over-the-body team movement.

Marni Brown and Einstein performing a turn-back between the legs.

*Melissa and Ally performing a back flip with a
transitional simultaneous spin of Melissa.*

Alena Smolivoka from the Czech Republic.

Melissa and Asah simultaneously jumping in a canine freestyle dancing routine.

Lucka Schonova from the Czech Republic.

Misa Androva from the Czech Republic.

Yva Androva from the Czech Republic.

Spin

1. Place your dog on an upside-down metal bucket.

2. Place a treat on your dog's nose. With your dog at 6 o'clock, turn your hand from 6 to 9 to 12 to 3 and back to 6. Go slow enough so your dog can follow the food and then reward back 6.

3. Do not forget to add the word "spin," which is a clockwise spin of 360 degrees. Make sure that you ask for one spin and then reward for a while. Then increase to two spins, then three spins.

4. Slowly phase out your big hand signals and use just a flash of a hand to the left for a spin.

Glory performing a spin on a tree stump, which you can use instead of a metal bucket.

Whirl

1. Follow the same instructions for a spin (see above), but move the treat counterclockwise and say "whirl."

Glory getting ready to perform a Whirl.

Back Up

1. The easiest method for teaching your dog to back up to so use a hallway.

2. Walk into your dog and flash your hands, with the back of your hands facing your dog and say "back."

3. Reward if your dog backs. If not, then walk back yourself and ask the dog "front" and reward. Then step into your dog again and say "back."

4. Try this several times, stepping into your dog's space a little more. You should get him back sooner or later.

5. You can also place food on your dog's nose and gently push the treat into your dog face while gently pushing him back.

6. Once your dog is backing up, ask more steps backward. The quickest way to get a response is to walk into him and have him back up. It usually works to get the dog started quickly as dog's understand livestock pressure, in which walking into an animal puts pressure on, and walking back or turning away takes the pressure off.

Asah backing up during a canine freestyle dancing performance.

Weave

Weaving in and out of your legs is a fun exercise and a nice transitional movement in and out of tricks and segments.

1. With your dog on your left side in a close position, step with your right leg forward, and lure your dog with food between your legs.

2. Then step with your left leg and lure your dog between them again while stepping forward.

3. Reward your dog each time and continue to repeat.

4. Don't forget to give the command "weave."

Glory also loves to weave.

Stand Tall

This is a great way to build muscle and strengthen our dog's rear end.

1. Hold a treat on your dog's nose and slowly raise the food letting the dog lick the food as he stands up.

2. If you have to, you can help your dog balance by holding one of his legs, but I prefer not to get stuck holding my dog's leg and move on quickly to them standing on their own.

Donna Schoech and Diva performing a multiple shuffle in a stand tall.

Shake Hands

1. With food in your right hand pick up your dog's left paw, and give him a treat with that same hand.

2. Extend your left hand out and repeat that exercise with food in your left hand picking up your dog's right foot.

3. Give a command like "left" and "right."

4. A quicker way to teach shake is to lift your dog's right paw with your left hand and say "shake" and then feed him his dinner. You can then expand and ask for "shake left" and "shake right" separately before dinner and, boy, watch him learn that much quicker!

Tanner Williams and Edward shaking hands.

Viola is taking shaking hands at another level.

Roll Over

Teaching your dog the "roll over" command is important because if your dog ever tumbles while running, he will know that he can roll out. Plus, it's a cute trick.

1. Place a treat on your dog's nose when he is lying on his side.

2. Move the treat so the dog has to roll out of the down the opposite way he is lying. So if the dog is lying on his right side, start with the treat on his nose and roll it across his chin from his right to his left.

3. You can help him roll over by gently rolling his front legs over and when the dog has rolled over on his left side, gently roll the treat on the ground in his view, away from his body so he will want to roll out of the trick.

Foot Stall

There are several ways to teach a foot stall, but the simplest way is to make a small rectangular board out of plywood and attach two strings close to the end of the left and right side of the board. This should be far enough apart so your feet can fit in between the two strings.

1. Lie on your back with your feet on the board (holding the strings for balance), and have a second person (standing beside you) lure your dog up onto the board, or just have her place the dog up on the board the first few times.

2. The trick is to teach your dog to load up, giving a "feet" command, and let your dog right on the board up from an angle in front of his face to your straight-legged position.

3. Eventually you can lie down without the board and your dog should transfer the "feet" command.

4. One of the most important things you need to do when your dog is comfortably balancing on your feet is have a second person gently remove one of his feet and let the dog replace his foot back onto your feet. This teaches your dog how to balance and adjust.

5. One way to prepare my dog for the foot stall is to teach him to jump onto a tree stump.

6. If you do not have any tree stumps, you can also try this other method, which I developed. Place two six-by-six pressure-treated landscape timbers in the ground at two different heights and use that.

Laura Moretz and Riot perform a foot stall.

Back Stall

1. The best way to teach a back stall is for you to kneel on all fours yourself.

2. Have a second person stand on your right side and lure the dog up onto your back with a treat.

3. Your goal is to have the person kneeling command the dog to "load up" and then lure and reward the dog.

4. To get the dog comfortable, have the second person walk from side to side once the dog is already on your back.

5. Switch to one-person commanding while still on all fours. Reward by reaching your hand back around.

6. It is important for your dog to always load up on the same side. I have my dogs load up from right to left or from front to back as I do not have them vault in any of those positions.

Melissa and Glory demonstrating a back stall.

Lourdes and Cisco, World Finals First Runner-Up. Lourdes is the first person create and perform a back stall to a beg and a multiple.

Turn Back Through Your Legs

For this trick you can use a disc, toy, or treat.

1. With your dog facing you, take the treat from the dog's nose, at 6 o'clock, and move your hand to 3 and 12.

2. When your hand gets to 12, gently push the treat back into your dog's nose. Start rewarding when the dog takes one or two steps.

3. Then increase the steps back he must do to get the treat. Your goal is that your dog understands the command, "turn back," and have your dog back up all the way through your legs and come out the back.

4. Do not start moving to your dog as he will never learn to turn himself in a 180-degree turn and turn to the middle of your legs.

5. For proficiency, walk backward a little, while your dog is walking back. Your dog must learn rear-end awareness and to drive backward with his rear legs.

Marni Brown and Einstein Turn back through.

Kick off the Body

There are many ways to teach a kick off the body, but the most successful is luring the dog with a treat with the dog starting in front of you.

1. Bring the treat from his nose area to your body quickly, luring him from left to right of your body ending with you luring him down, so he looks for his landing.

2. In the beginning, lure him from your left hip to your right shoulder by making a circle behind the dog's head after he has jumped up and touched your body. You want the dog to place all four feet on your body to push off, but at the beginning reward anything and then ask for more feet for the reward.

3. This is all about trust and luring properly, and if the dog lands but does not complete a full circle turning counterclockwise, then make the dog turn counterclockwise before giving him a treat for attempting the trick.

4. Here is a trick I learned when my little dog Faith learned to kick with jumping up and only pushing off with her one right front paw. Raising my left leg to the right side of the front of my body made her have to jump over my leg and touch my torso, which in turn, made her use four feet. Now, two things were different the day she learned to kick with all four feet. One, I raised my leg across my body, but two, I also had a large winter coat on, and it gave her a much larger platform to push off of. She is now consistently kicking with all four feet.

Teaching a kick off the body.

Lucka Schonova and Dixi from the Czech Republic.

Monomi Konishi and Liaka demonstrating a kick off the chest.

Over the Body

1. The secret of performing an over is, as a general rule, to start throwing the disc in one flight plane directly over your body.

2. Start your dog from a close position and work your way up to a running over. Make sure that you throw the disc in a consistent place and height for the dog, and make sure the throw is early enough so the dog knows how high to jump to catch the disc.

3. As your dog advances, you can start to throw the disc in two planes of flight over your body and release the disc two to five disc lengths away from the center of your body on the landing side of the dog's running path. This teaches your dog to hang longer and even stretch in the air to catch the disc.

4. There are only a few exceptions when I will throw in front of my body for an over. Generally I only recommend this when you have a dog that continues to hit your leg or body on the ascending part of the jump.

Melissa and Ally performing a hurdle from back to front.

Melissa and Asah demonstrating a flat over-the-body maneuver.

Monami Konishi and Liaka performing a hurdle from front to back.

Melissa and Asah performing an over-the-body from head to toe.

Marni Brown and Quin demonstrating a hurdle over the body.

Melissa and Faith over-the-body while lying flat.

Creating Segments and a Freestyle Routine

What tricks flow well together? Place tricks together that flow from right to left and left to right as well as from front to back and back to front. Whenever I create a routine, I also pick the starting position on the field by the wind direction. So, each trick has a preferred wind direction, and each following trick needs to take the dog's placement, disc placement, and current wind direction in mind. Just remember to vary your send outs while you pick up discs. A perfect routine is one where the judges never notice the player pick up a disc and especially do not see the dog waiting for the player to find and pick up any discs in disc management.

SAMPLE ROUTINE

An easy way to remember your routine is to outline it, and once your segments are set, only recall and remember the first word in each segment. Also, create a laminated card with each description on each side of the card and place it in your bag.

Mel & Asah

- Circle, spin
- Hurdle
  - Over leg
  - Over shoulder
- Flip Left
  - Flip
  - Flip
  - Flip
  - Upside down wrist flip
- Behind back
  - Air bounce
  - Behind back
  - Air bounce
  - Under leg
- Spin flip
  - Over body
  - Upside down
  - Two hand
  - Push

- Upside down
  - Side arm
  - Air bounce
  - Behind back
  - Overhand wrist flip spin
- Flip shuffle
  - Flip shuffle
  - Flip shuffle
  - Flip shuffle
  - Flip dog catch
- Flip catch Asah starts between legs

Conclusion

One of my goals in life is to teach pet owners that their dogs do not have to be a burden, but can be active and willing family members. Instead of banishing your dog to the backyard, try a simple game of fetch. It changed my dogs' lives, and I hope it will do the same for yours.

An important factor for future pet owners to consider is adopting a pet. My father taught me responsible horse and dog breeding, but he also instilled in me that every responsible animal breeder is also an avid animal rescuer. However, the most important thing my father taught me was that being a responsible animal rescuer did not mean personally rescuing every animal oneself, but instead finding a way to adopt, help, and give one's time as much as possible for any animal in need. So, helping people adopt the pet that fits their personality and lifestyle is the most important thing I have learned about helping homeless pets.

One a side note, my little rescue dog, Viola, a red cattle dog mix, was a homeless dog living on the streets. She was one of those dogs that everyone would shoo away. Viola was very difficult in the rescue organization, and they were worried they would never find a home for the troublemaker of a dog who was so busy, very vocal, extremely destructive, and just all-round difficult. After evaluating her, I knew she would be a challenge, but because she loved to use her feet and mouth, I knew she should make a great disc dog. The rest is history. Little Viola went from terror to trained, and homeless to celebrity, traveling around the U.S. helping raise money and awareness for other homeless pets. And she is a wonderful member of the family.

Viola and Melissa at Flying Dog Field.

Viola and Melissa ending a performance promoting rescue dogs.

Dedication

Friends . . . Companions . . . and Saying Goodbye

To my Dad, Dorcey. You were passionate in life, you loved and preserved nature, and you enjoyed giving and helping anyone in need. From a young farm boy to a deputized mounted sheriff, from a scenic traveler to the best companion a daughter would ever have, you were the most honorable man, horse trainer, father, and teacher of values ever to grace this wonderful earth. You have touched this world like no other. I love you and miss you.

Dorcey Groulx
May 1939 ~ December 2009

Cody, my first Border Collie, your intelligence and boredom allowed me to change my hobby and passion for training animals into a career. More than two decades ago, after you chewed a hole in my couch and learned to open the pantry door (and then shook all the dry goods all over my living room), I first picked up a flying disc to entertain you. That moment allowed me to change my way of life and career path.

Cody, the Cunning Border Collie
December 24, 1988 ~ December 24, 2002

To Ariel Asah, World Champion partner, you were not just a great Disc Dog you were my best friend and companion. Asah you were a healthy, energetic partner, and for more than thirteen years you always gave it your all. I miss you.

Ariel Asah, World Champion
March 23, 1995 ~ February 2, 2009

My heart weighs, so heavy having to say goodbye again so soon to my Disc Dog, Friend, Companion, and Partner . . . Ariel Ally. On Oct 31, 2010, Ariel Ally, the Florida State Champion and daughter of World Champion Ariel Asah, passed away unexpectedly. Saying goodbye is so difficult. Ally, you touched my life in so many wonderful ways . . . rest in peace.

Ariel Ally, Florida State Champion
January 7, 1999 ~ Oct 31, 2010

Photo Credits

Steven Donahue, See Spot Run Photography There are many professional photographers who see the wildly entertaining sport of canine disc and try their hand at photographing our sport. However, only a very few photographers are as skilled at this amazing sport as Steven Donahue of See Spot Run Photography. So I hope you enjoy some of Steven Donahue's work in this book. Don't forget to check out his website, www.seespotrunphoto.com.

Other photos in this book are courtesy of: David Herrin, Pavel Humpolec, http://fotohack.cz, Tomasz Monko, http://k9action.eu, Dan Phillips, www.worldofdogsports.com, Hiro Saki, and Lucka Schonova, www.darri.chodskypes.eu.

For More Information

For all of your canine disc and human flying discs and accessories, visit Discovering the World at www.dtworld.com. Dan Mangone, owner of DTW, has been producing canine and human discs for over more than three decades, and whether you're looking for an inexpensive marketing giveaway or a competition dog disc, Dan's your man.

The U.S. Disc Dog Nationals International Steering Committee (USDDN SC, www.usddn.com) is the only disc dog organization run by the players for the players with over thirty experienced players worldwide. The USDDN was created 2000 by several club representatives in the U.S. and started the National Finals in 2001. It is the only disc dog organization who certifies judges worldwide, created a judging handbook, and allows competitors a voice through their club or country representative. The USDDN SC opened the Steering Committee to international country representatives in 2005 and has been growing worldwide ever since. One of the most important things the USDDN SC has done was promote canine safety and create a code of conduct. Even today, the USDDN SC is the only organization to penalize and define structured penalties for unsafe tricks under the Canine Endangerment Rule. In my opinion, the Canine Endangerment Rule is one of the most important rules any canine organization can have. The USDDN hosts a series of locals, qualifiers, and a world finals tournament for beginners and weekend warriors. The USDDN SC encourages individuals, parks and recreation departments, and local dog clubs of any kind to get involved with hosting a fun-filled family toss & fetch competition. You can request an electronic competition form kit to host your very own local toss & fetch competition at www.usddn.com. Over all, the USDDN is about offering a fun and safe tournament, which is how our canine disc sport can continue to grow, but it is also dedicated to creating the most effective rules and judging criteria for crowning a Toss & Fetch and Freestyle Disc Dog World Champion.

Dan Phillips of www.worldofdogsports.com is a website you will want to bookmark. If you want to learn any dog sport, visit Dan's website for your favorite dog training DVD. As one of my official photographers and as photographer for the USDDN Disc Dog World Finals, he is also the official live-stream dog sports expert. You can always find an intriguing dog sports competition to watch.

My Dog's Milestones

Day 1
_____
_____
_____
_____

Day 2
_____
_____
_____

Day 3
_____
_____
_____

Day 4
_____
_____
_____

Day 5
_____
_____
_____

Day 6
_____
_____

Day 7

Day 8

Day 9

Day 10

Day 11

Day 12

Day 13

Day 14

Day 15

Day 16

Day 17

Day 18

About the Author

In 1997, Melissa Heeter made history with her dog, Ariel Asah, by becoming the first woman to win the Canine Disc World Championships title. Since winning, Melissa was also the first woman to set the outdoor and indoor canine disc distance records, and has dedicated her life to teaching pet owners how to have fun, play safe, and strengthen their bond with their dogs through a simple game of fetch.

In addition, Melissa produces six of the largest disc dog tournaments in the world, and travels around the U.S., Canada, Czech Republic, Germany, Japan, the Netherlands, Poland, and South America performing, instructing how-to seminars, and judging worldwide. She is the USDDN Steering Committee International Judging Director and had created the first canine disc judging certification program.

Find out more about Melissa Heeter and WOOF! Sports USA at www.woofsports.com.

About Cider Mill Press
Book Publishers

Good ideas ripen with time. From seed to harvest, Cider Mill Press brings fine reading, information, and entertainment together between the covers of its creatively crafted books. Our Cider Mill bears fruit twice a year, publishing a new crop of titles each spring and fall.

Visit us on the Web at
www.cidermillpress.com
or write to us at
12 Port Farm Road
Kennebunkport, Maine 04046